THE DEVIL IS IN THE DETAILS

J. HAMILTON WESTON

Energion Publications
Gonzalez, FL
2018

eBook Editions:
Aer.io: 978-1-63199-575-0
Kindle: 978-1-63199-576-7
iBooks: 978-1-63199-577-4
Google Play: 978-1-63199-578-1

Print Edition
ISBN10: 1-63199-540-5
ISBN13: 978-1-63199-540-8
Library of Congress Control Number: 2018950123

Energion Publications
P. O. Box 841
Gonzalez, FL 32560
energionpubs.com
pubs@energion.com
850-525-3916

I would like to acknowledge my Lord and Savior Jesus Christ
for His inspiration in the writing of this book.
It is in the power of the knowledge provided to me
by the Holy Spirit in my life
that strength is given to me to complete it for Him.

TABLE OF CONTENTS

1   The Church at Ephesus: Good, but Lacking Love..........1

2   The Church at Smyrna: The Poor, but Rich Church....13

3   Pergamos: The Deceitful Compromise.....................25

4   The Church in Thyatira: Jezebel's House.....................41

5   Sardis: The Dead Church.....................................55

6   Philadelphia: The Loyal and Faithful............................67

7   Laodicea: The Luke Warm Church 79

8   The Spiritual Church:
A Call Back to the True Spiritual Beginnings...............93

9   Is the Bride of Christ Ready for the Bridegroom? 107

INTRODUCTION

John, to the seven churches
which are in Asia:

Grace to you and peace from Him who is and
who was and who is to come, and from the seven
Spirits who are before His throne, and from Jesus
Christ, the faithful witness, the firstborn from
the dead, and the ruler
over the kings of the earth.
(Revelation 1:4-5)

I am sure that the church at which I presently pastor is probably thinking, by now, that I am thoroughly obsessed with the study of the Beatitudes. Maybe this is justified. But, I think that there is not enough studied or even preached concerning Jesus' teachings in His first sermon. The belief that the life of the Believer is solely given to one moment in time, then the work is complete, and from that point on, is on God, is probably one of the most effective deceptions the Adversary ever devised. The acceptance of the salvation of our souls that rests in God's hands tells us that we do not have to worry because He is handling everything is another part of the deception. Our salvation rests in the understanding of how we can truly serve the Lord with all our hearts and love one another as He has loved us. What does that really mean?

The seven churches addressed in the book of Revelation gives the reader a glimpse behind the veil. It should be noted, from the beginning, that the reader needs to enter the study of the revelations of Jesus as not only directed to the churches in that area at that time. He is addressing the churches of today. Just as Jesus is described as the one who was and who is and always will be, these are relevant to even the churches today. The deception is seen in that the modern-day church is led into the belief that the book of Revelation was only relevant for those seven churches and only during that time. This is truly false!

The church today believes that this is a new day for Believers and that they are taking a new direction. This is because of the belief that all things of the Bible are old and are looked upon as stories not relevant for today's church. The one presenting the vision to John as a revelation for all people to the seven churches is identified as Jesus Christ Himself. He reinforces this declaration by stating that He is the faithful witness, the first born from the dead, and the ruler of the kings of the earth. These titles need to be noted for consideration because we know John must have recognized Him. John was the one disciple who not only was present when Jesus died on the cross, but he was also witness to His resurrection and ascension. Jesus was making the reader aware of His eternal credentials as a way of recording His authority for all time. Humanity, in all their arrogance and pride, need to realize their place in the presence of the living eternal person of Jesus Christ.

To Him who loved us and washed us from our
sins in His own blood, and has made us kings
and priests to His God and Father, to Him be
glory and dominion forever and ever. Amen.
(Revelation 1:5b-6)

This description of Jesus should reveal to the reader the intention of the book for the Believer. The one who lives in the gray areas of Christian belief would not understand what is being said in this incredible vision. Reading the entirety of the work, one would probably think that John was on some hallucinogen. But, to the one who truly seeks after the face of God in all their life, they will see the truth and beauty found within the vision. The revelation of our Lord Jesus Christ to the Apostle John, in my opinion, is not studied and taken to heart enough. As it says at the end of verse six, to Him be the glory and dominion forever and ever. This statement includes us. We are, whether Christians choose to accept it, among those who fall in the category of forever. For the first century church, they could not see past their century. This was because of the persecution widespread in their time. Regardless of the emperor, there was persecution in one form or another, from one Roman province or another. Christians in that time prepared for the inevitable way of existence and ultimately death.

There are many countries today where Christians endure persecution on a massive scale. Are we as children of God called to stand and be proactive? Are we not to be involved until we are backed into a corner? Then, are we to be always reactive, never on the offensive but always on the defensive? Are we to look the other way and allow the adversary to make a foothold in the world? How do you understand the Christian life and why? These are questions that need to be considered when truly evaluating your spiritual health. Do you look forward to your time with the Lord or does it become a drudgery or obligation? It is true. This book may not seem more inspired than any other on the surface. But, we are going to look deep into the true mission and vision of the church. We will look at the earliest ideals set in place by Jesus Himself when He taught His first sermon on the mountainside in Matthew Chapters 5 – 7. This will be carried into the future church of not only the first century, but even today's church. There needs to be an understanding of intent to fully appreciate the anarchical mess found in Christianity today.

---

*I was in the Spirit on the Lord's Day, and I
heard behind me a loud voice, as of a trumpet,
saying, "I am the Alpha and the Omega, the*

*First and the Last," and, "What you see, write in
a book and send it to the seven churches which
are in Asia: to Ephesus, to Smyrna, to Pergamos,
to Thyatira, to Sardis, to Philadelphia, and to
Laodicea."* (Revelation 1:10-11)

The commission that is given to John was one that sent him far beyond anything he had ever experienced. He had a relationship with the Lord Jesus that none of the other disciples shared. He was given charge by a dying Jesus on the cross to care for Mary, His mother. There was something special about John. He came to John, not because he was the only Apostle living but he was the one who could carry the message without wavering or compromise. Jesus knew that John would lay down his own life for the task to be complete. In the first ten verses of the book of Revelation, John not only establishes his credibility with the reader. But, he also introduces the Lord Jesus in His glory, honor and praise as well as the authority that is due Him.

When Jesus gave the disciples the Beatitudes as a standard to aim for and live by, they did not truly grasp the entirety of His meaning until He poured out on them the Holy Spirit and they received Him. At that moment, the light came into their lives and they finally understood all the things that the Lord Jesus had tried to teach them. We have the Word of God at our finger tips. Are we willing to take the Words of the "Alpha and Omega" and the "Beginning and the End" and make Him real to a lost and sinful world? Jesus said that He came to save those who are lost.

*... and in the midst of the seven lampstands One
like the Son of Man, clothed with a garment
down to the feet and girded about the chest with
a golden band. His head and hair were white
like wool, as white as snow, and His eyes like a*

flame of fire; His feet were like fine brass, as if
refined in a furnace, and His voice as the sound
of many waters;   (Revelation 1:13-15)

The vision is much for the first century person to absorb. For John, he recognized Him as the Son of Man, but He was in His glorified state. What beauty he beheld and majesty as Jesus walked among the seven lampstands. The Glory of the Father in the only begotten Son. John recognized Him too because he had been taken up in the Spirit. The power of the Holy Spirit at work in John was evident in the manner and suddenness of which John was taken. This happened as if it had occurred before. For the Believer to truly receive all that the book of Revelation gives, one must be willing to accept the fact that the Holy Spirit is real and at work not only in the individual but in the church too. The Beatitudes hold just as true for the Body of Christ as much as it does for each member of the Body.

For as the body is one and has many mem-
bers, but all the members of that one body,
being many, are one body, so also is Christ. For
by one Spirit we were all baptized into one
body—whether Jews or Greeks, whether slaves or
free—and have all been made to drink into one
Spirit. For in fact the body is not one member
but many. (I Corinthians 12:12-14)

Consider for a moment how far off the rails Christianity has gone. How much has modern Christians become complacent with chaos and sin in the world. Much of what is seen on cable and the internet is rationalized by saying that there is just as much good out there as is evil. This may be true. But what are we willing to let into our homes and, even worse, into the church. God's own house!

I have said from the pulpit and in teachings and many meetings that we are more willing to usher the adversary through the doors of the church and even into the pulpits in the name of Jesus and compassion, than we are those who desire and seek the Lord. Why? Because, as fallen humans, there is more of a tendency to follow lies rather than the truth.

The Apostle Paul experienced this first hand. The sooner he would establish a body of true Believers, then a faction of false teachers within the body of Believers would rise to twist the truth to cater to their desires. Today's church is no different. Today it is on a much larger scale. If the church and all its members would look to the Beatitudes for their strength in their growth in sanctification, the church would then begin to grow in a positive and God-like manner. The church grows in number but not in souls who look to Christ alone and rely on fully the Holy Spirit for guidance and strength. It is only through the power of the Holy Spirit, which binds the Body as one, that the church in all its diversity can work and live as one. That was the intent from the beginning.

The question probably asked by those who read the book of Revelation is the most obvious. Why? Why would a loving God who would go so far as sending His Only Son as a sacrifice so a fallen and sinful, evil humanity could be reconciled to Him? Because of Free Will, He has given fallen humanity the opportunity to make the right choices. Throughout history, humanity has made major and crucial wrong choices and have taken the wrong paths, but in all the wrong that has been done, even in His name, He still sees a right spirit. A light that remains in the darkness. The book of Revelation is a wake-up call not only for the non-believer, but it is a real awakening for the Believer. Remember, Jesus said that there will be many who come in His name saying "Lord, Lord!" and He said that He will say to them "Depart from Me for I never knew you." Do you want the Lord Jesus Christ to say those words to you when you stand before the throne of God?

As this examination of the church opens to the reader, my prayer is that we can enter in the conversation with an open mind and heart to be willing receive what the Holy Spirit is wanting to teach the church but assist the Believer in their growth down the path of sanctification. I believe that the reader shall begin to fully understand the workings of the Holy Spirit and His relation to the church. Then, the Believer can more fully relate and be strengthened in their own walk with Christ in the power of the Holy Spirit. The Believer in Christ Jesus as savior must keep in mind that the Beatitudes and the letters to the seven churches in Asia Minor are inevitably linked because the Father, Son, and the Holy Spirit are One. As they are one, so the church will be one. But, the church must first take responsibility and accept the work of the Holy Spirit and allow the Spirit to cleanse the Body of Christ from all unrighteousness. Is the Bride of Christ ready for the Bridegroom? We shall see!

Let us Pray;

O Most Gracious Heavenly Father, I seek your cleansing in my life. Lord, make me worthy to stand in Your presence. Make pure and holy so that I can serve You with all my heart. You are my Savior and my God. There is none like You and it is to Your Glory that I Pray. Lord, I seek Your wisdom in all things and I receive the guidance and strengthening of Your Holy Spirit in my life that I may serve You will all my heart, mind, soul, and strength and that I may love others as You have loved me. In the of the Father, The Son, and the Holy Spirit. In Jesus Name, Amen.

CHAPTER I

THE CHURCH AT EPHESUS: GOOD, BUT LACKING LOVE

Nevertheless I have this against you, that you have left your first love. Remember therefore from where you have fallen; repent and do the first works, or else I will come to you quickly and re-move your lampstand from its place—unless you repent. (Revelation 2:4-5)

The belief that we are "once saved always saved" is a true mis-understanding of the infallible Word of God. Many branches of the Christian faith stand by this very notion and are deceived by their own weak knowledge of Scripture and by the subtle false teachings spread within the church today. This concept also gives way to the idea that a person cannot ever lose their salvation or that the Spirit of God cannot ever be removed from them. The nation of Israel, God's own chosen people, experienced this several times over their extensive, complex and troubled history. In the Old Testament, there are countless stories of Israel's faithfulness followed by their inability to follow God's simple directions while His presence is visible to them. We, as God's chosen also or Christians, tend to place judgments on Israel and wonder why they are unable to see the forest for the trees. But, Christians today live in much the same blurred vision of God.

The Revelation of Jesus Christ to the church in Ephesus intro-duces one of the subtle ironies in the church today. As much as the Christians, in the United States, especially today, see themselves as all on the fast track to the pearly gates. This is a grave deception.

The misunderstanding is found in the thought that once you go to the altar and give yourself to the Lord to save you, then all the requirements are fulfilled. The next step is to become active and productive little church people. Many very active and productive churches follow this mentality. There are very few of these churches who have a high percentage of membership who are truly active. The truth is that the larger the membership, the smaller the group of active participants in the ministries of the church. These churches are, on the surface, in touch with the people and their needs. They are not only in touch with the community, but also with the needs of those in church as well.

So, the question is asked, "Is not this a good thing?" Yes! On the surface, everything seems to be going down the path to righteousness and eternal glory. But, there lies subtle problems. Some are seen and addressed and some are left to dissolve on their own. In the church at Ephesus, Jesus told them that they were very virtuous as a body of Believers and sound in their doctrines, but even they lacked something they needed. As this chapter unfolds, we will look deep into the heart of the problems found in the church of Ephesus and the relationship it mirrors to the churches today. We will consider how Jesus instructs us to correct it and truly live a righteous life before a Holy God. Remember, God is not the one who turned away from us, but we are the ones who have turned away from Him to our own devices.

EPHESUS: CHURCH OF WORKS AND SOUND DOCTRINE

I know thy works, and thy labor, and thy patience, and how thou canst not bear them which are evil: and thou hast tried them which say they are apostles, and are not, and hast found them liars: And hast borne, and hast patience, and for

*my name's sake hast labored, and hast not faint-
ed.* (Revelation 2:2-3)

The city of Ephesus was a very prosperous city during the time that Jesus spoke to the Apostle John in Revelation. Ephesus was a wealthy port city noted as a major trade port for those going in and out of Asia Minor. The city was a strategic place for the spread of the gospel of Christ. The people were extremely open to the Gospel and the church founded there by Paul and Barnabas flourished and grew substantially during the two years that they were there. As can be noted in Scripture, those who founded the churches in Colossae, as well as those of the other six churches of Revelation, were most probably born from those who were under Paul's ministry in Ephesus.

The Ephesian church, as shown by Christ to John, was still the faithful, virtuous, and strong doctrinal church that Paul began fifty years earlier. They even exhibited many of the gifts of the Spirit. When Paul was imprisoned while in Rome following the third missionary journey, he spent over two years ministering to the people of Asia Minor. Ephesus was a hub for financial, import and export, and religious centers for the entire region. Especially, concerning the religious trepidations because Jews and Gentiles alike believed and were baptized in the name of the Lord Jesus Christ under the teachings of Paul and the empowering of the Holy Spirit. Much of these characteristics were evident in the days of John as seen in the vision. John, per tradition, also had a strong following in Ephesus. But, as Paul did, John also grated against the raw nerve of some of the officials and business people of the day. This landed him in prison as well.

The Church's strong stances stood against and called out those who spoke evil against the teachings concerning Jesus as the Christ. There were those within the city who dedicated their lives to attempting to destroying those who followed Jesus. In the letter to the Ephesian church, Paul wrote primarily about unity of the church equating with the oneness of the Spirit, Christ, and the Father. This is a thread that is woven throughout the letter and is common in most of his other letters as well. Apparently, Jesus saw these qualities evidenced in the church.

The churches of today that resemble the Ephesian church are small to medium sized churches that are strong in belief and doctrine. They can border on the line of fanatical, as understood in some circles. These congregations are very active in community action and usually have the appearance of an open-door policy. There are always programs occurring on a regular basis on the church property. Primarily, these activities are designed to draw the hurting and the lost to the church. They also get involved in social action groups within the community. These are all good in and of themselves. But, the problem comes when the church seeks its own glory and not the glory of God in all it does. So, when we consider the way the world works in relation to the church and its authority, there needs to be understood the notion that just because it appears to be good and feels right does not mean that it is right in the eyes of God.

Nevertheless, I have somewhat against thee, because thou hast left thy first love.
(Revelation 2:4)

The church in Ephesus had been active for more than fifty years by the time Jesus appeared to John in this vision. If we look back and consider Jesus' first teachings in Matthew Chapter 5, there can be understood more clearly what stood at the heart of Jesus' concern for this church. Even though the people of Ephesus were not physically present while Jesus presented His Sermon on the Mount, the church itself and those in the church were taught the fundamental basis for their faith by those who were there. Namely, John and those following him. When Jesus made this observation concerning the Ephesian church in Revelation Chapter 2, John knew full well what He was talking about and why He made such a statement. Jesus set a faith growing and sanctifying path for the Believer to follow. The Beatitudes were the standard for spiritual growth in the life of those who truly sought after God with all their hearts. Jesus was telling His followers that salvation was not just one event in a person's life. But, salvation is the entire life of the Believer.

The Ephesian church was extremely effective in many ways concerning outreach and understanding the pulse of the world around them, but it was all for their glory and not for God's glory. The church forgot what it meant to be humble before God. They forgot what it meant to be truly repentant daily. Pouring their hearts out to God. They were going through the motions but not believing and living them with their hearts. How is this any different than many of the churches today. Many have built for themselves mighty crystal cathedrals for the world to admire. God sees these as filthy rags! If it isn't done to the glory of God, then it is nothing.

When we are trying to grasp the notion of what it means to have lost their first love, think about yourself and the most loving and beautiful relationship you have ever experienced. Let say it was your first relationship. Your first kiss. You never forget that moment and that time in your life. It is the loss of your first love. From that time forward, you strive to attain that same experience in your life, but nothing truly measures to that relationship. Jesus is telling the Ephesian church and us today, remember what it was like when Jesus first came into your life. How overwhelmingly you were in love. For the Believer to truly live the godly life toward holiness, one must live everyday as if they are living that first time over again forever. The church of Ephesus had lost their focus because they had forgotten the place from which they had come.

THE BEGINNINGS OF MINISTRY IN EPHESUS

So Paul still remained a good while. Then he took leave of the brethren and sailed for Syria,

and Priscilla and Aquila were with him. He had
his hair cut off at Cenchrea, for he had taken
a vow. And he came to Ephesus, and left them
there; but he himself entered the synagogue and
reasoned with the Jews.
(Acts 18:18-19)

Paul, being a former Pharisee and now an Apostle of Jesus Christ, was given those into his charge by the Holy Spirit to establish various church throughout the empire. The Word of God began to spread quickly and through Paul's commitment and obedience to the Holy Spirit that certain Godly people were put in his path. The Lord gave Paul the guidance he needed to set those in place for the gospel to powerfully spread. It was a mixture of individual people with a variety of gifts. For example, Aquilla and Pricilla were a husband and wife team who forced out of Rome and connected with Paul in Corinth. From there, Paul trained them while at Corinth in the power of the Spirit. Once they arrived in the port of Ephesus, he helped establish the church and left them in charge. He went on to preach in the synagogue, as per his tradition.

Later, upon his return to Ephesus, there will be seen an increase of growth in that church. From there will spring forth other various churches in the whole of Asia Minor because of Paul's obedience to the Holy Spirit. Aquilla and Pricilla remained and the church at Ephesus flourished in the Lord. The next phase of the growth and leadership of Aquilla and Pricilla came with their encounter with an Alexandrian Jewish Christian named Apollos.

Now a certain Jew named Apollos, born at Al-
exandria, an eloquent man and mighty in the
Scriptures, came to Ephesus. This man had been
instructed in the way of the Lord; and being
fervent in spirit, he spoke and taught accurately
the things of the Lord, though he knew only the

baptism of John.
(Acts 18:24-25)

He was a product of the massive scattering of Jews and Christians alike to various portions of the empire. Alexandria Egypt was the religious base for those in the southern part of the kingdom. Apollos, per accounts, was knowledgeable in the ways of the Lord Jesus, but only familiar with the baptism of the John the Baptist, not the baptism of Jesus and the Holy Spirit. He genuinely sought the Lord and was a well-versed teacher. Aquilla and Pricilla took him in and taught him concerning the teaching and ways of the Lord Jesus Christ and the baptism of the Holy Spirit and church began to grow.

So he began to speak boldly in the synagogue.
When Aquila and Priscilla heard him, they took
him aside and explained to him the way of God
more accurately.
(Acts 18:26)

The various beginnings of any church had at its foundation its whole mission and vision rooted in the Holy Spirit and the teachings of the Lord Jesus Christ. In Ephesus, I believe the establishment of that church was geographically set as a central hub base for the remaining region. Remember, apart from the church in Colossae, there are no other letters to any other churches from that area. Then, Ephesus and six other churches are mentioned in the book of revelation. The only other mention of any of these churches, other than Ephesus, is mention in Paul's letter to the Colossians of the church at Laodicea. So, as can be seen, the church from the beginning played an important role for the spread of the gospel throughout the empire. The point that the Ephesian church was mentioned first among the seven churches in revelation shows its prominence among the others and the importance of that church to the spread of the Christian faith to the known world. Certain people, like Aquilla, Pricilla and Apollos, in addition to Paul, played vital roles in the over-all spread of the gospel.

The character of an individual is understood in terms of how they are viewed by those around them. Apollos was no different. And this probably helped some consistency to the foundation of the church in Ephesus.

---

*And when he desired to cross to Achaia, the
brethren wrote, exhorting the disciples to receive
him; and when he arrived, he greatly helped
those who had believed through grace; for he vigorously refuted the Jews publicly, showing from
the Scriptures that Jesus is the Christ.*
(Acts 18:27-28)

The Holy Spirit guided the walk of Aquilla and Pricilla into the path of Apollos. He was instructed and then prepared for further ministry in Greece or Achaia. There Apollos assisted in solidifying the ministry and various churches of that area. The point is that Apollos, Aquilla and Pricilla were all led by the Spirit of God and they even more vigorously pronounced and spread the gospel of Christ. The church continued because at its foundation was the love of Christ. They continued the spread of the gospel because they were living the Beatitudes taught by Christ in the beginning of His ministry.

THE LATER VIEW OF EPHESUS' SIGNIFICANCE THROUGH THE MINISTRY OF PAUL

---

*Therefore I also, after I heard of your faith in the
Lord Jesus and your love for all the saints, do not
cease to give thanks for you, making mention of*

you in my prayers:
(Ephesians 1:15-16)

The Apostle Paul had a certain place in his heart for the Ephesian church He was concerned for the factions that continued to twist the teachings and testimony of Jesus Christ in that area. As with any group of Christians, there are various opinions and ideals for the ways to which the gospel is taught. This is even evident in the church of today. The message is delivered in a way that appeals to those present. The methods are different, but message needs to be the same. Paul encountered a twisting of the truth of the gospel in most of the churches he and others with him helped established. With division in the churches because of these false teachers, the letter to the Ephesian church sought for a foundation in the love of Christ for one another. In this, the church, with its foundation in Christ's love, must unify and establish a oneness that reflects Christ in all their lives in and out the church.

---

*I, therefore, the prisoner of the Lord, beseech you
to walk worthy of the calling with which you
were called, with all lowliness and gentleness,
with longsuffering, bearing with one another in
love, endeavoring to keep the unity of the Spirit
in the bond of peace. There is one body and one
Spirit, just as you were called in one hope of your
calling; one Lord, one faith, one baptism; one
God and Father of all, who is above all, and
through all, and in you all.*
(Ephesians 4:1-6)

Even though this church had been faithful, it remained that it had lost the identity set in the moment Christ had become realized in the lives of those in Ephesus. Jesus said to John that the church in Ephesus was doing all the right things. But, there was only one thing they lack and that was they had lost their first love. When Paul was writing to that same church some forty years earlier, they were suffering from a lack of Spiritual empowerment. This meaning that they were doing all the right things and the church was expanding out to other cities in the province of Asia, but its focus and basis of their beliefs were dimming. This, in turn, was eventually the cause for division in the church. Paul wanted to encourage unity within the churches because there is strength in numbers and he saw this as their greatest asset. The Ephesian church was mentioned by Jesus as an example to other churches in the world to never forget where they came from in their faith. That is why we can look at the Ephesian church with encouragement and strength in today's leadership in congregations. Many churches lose their perspective and focus because of world and its influences and the subtle infiltration of the adversary.

HOW FAR ARE WE OFF TARGET?

> *He who has an ear, let him hear what the Spirit*
> *says to the churches. To him who overcomes I will*
> *give to eat from the tree of life, which is in the*
> *midst of the Paradise of God.*
> (Revelation 2:7)

The big question should be how do we overcome the adversary in our lives today? Remember and never forget the place from which you have come. This in turn will provide strength for the day and a vision for the future. The Lord Jesus saw this as basic and true for the beginning patterns and process of growth for the church. The church is only as strong as its members. The members are only as strong as the faith of the weakest member. So, as you consider the level of faith established within your congregation, maybe there needs to be more time spent on strengthening the weakest members and making them strong. Jesus spent most of His ministry with those who were outcast and down trotted. If we then go back to the moment we met Jesus and that love and peace that was overwhelming, then we will soon understand Jesus' concern with the Ephesian church and those of like ways and practices. Jesus said that if you do not go back to your first works and remember from where you have fallen, He will remove your lampstand. This means that He will remove His presence and blessings from that congregation and those who are part of it. How far have you fallen and do you have the faith necessary to regain that which you have lost?

TEACHING MOMENTS FROM EPHESUS

1. What should your church glean from reflection on the church in Ephesus?

2. How does this give you a new perspective on the way you conduct the affairs in and around your congregation?

3. How can your congregation improve their understanding of God's vision for your church?

4. Is Jesus Christ your first true love? If so, return to Him and rejoice in your salvation. If Jesus is not your Lord and Savior, seek Him first and grow with Him to eternity.

Let us Pray;

Heavenly Father, thank You for Your Most Gracious gift in Your Son and my Savior Jesus Christ. Help me, Lord, not to ever forget my first love and Your gift of salvation of my soul. You gave Your life that I may have eternal life. I am eternally indebted in love. In Jesus' Name, Amen.

CHAPTER 2

THE CHURCH AT SMYRNA: THE POOR, BUT RICH CHURCH

Do not fear any of those things which you are about to suffer. Indeed, the devil is about to throw some of you into prison, that you may be tested, and you will have tribulation ten days. Be faithful until death, and I will give you the crown of life. (Revelation 2:10)

The understanding of persecution found within the church cannot be fully grasped in today's Americanized society. The church in America today lives in a bubble of their own creation. Within the bubble, we develop our own definition of reality. The church in ancient Smyrna was no different. The difference is that they stood firm in times of the persecution. Smyrna was a city of great wealth and influence in the ancient Roman province of Asia Minor. This historic city, even in the first century, because it is noted for its historic and notable individuals. The poet Homer, writer of the famous writings of *The Odyssey* and *The Illiad*. The infamous story of the war between the Greek states and the city of Troy over the famous Helen. Also, the history of the city accredits Alexander the Great for establishing the city as a cultural and trade center and therefore setting it up as one of the wealthiest cities in Asia Minor. Smyrna was noted for its sale and trade perfumes and myrrh.

The city of Smyrna, like that of Ephesus relied on international trade for its wealth. But, the driving force that guided every aspect of their society was religion. The belief in something that more in control of their lives was at the heart of their culture. This was due to the influences of Alexander the Great. The Hellenism or Greek counter-culture that took root and gave rise to many superstitions which for pagan religions. The church in Smyrna had within it the converts from these pagan belief systems. The church received much of their persecution from those pagan people who felt their systematic way of life was threatened. Much like today in the world and society. The world feels threatened because of what Christianity offers is something they cannot give but they choose to destroy it. This church, according to how the Lord Jesus says concerning them, is not only going through but will go through much in terms of persecution. The church at Smyrna seems to be the church is going to endure much suffering because of the opening verse. He tells the angel and the church not to fear. The emotion that holds a grip on most people and causes them not to do what they want to do, is fear. The Apostle Paul wrote in his letter to the Roman church;

For we know that the law is spiritual, but I am
carnal, sold under sin. For what I am doing, I
do not understand. For what I will to do, that I
do not practice; but what I hate, that I do.
(Romans 7:14-15)

Paul had a struggle that had him bound to the law of sin and death. The struggle with sin is one everybody deals with daily. The church at Smyrna would be no different. But, Jesus saw the church as they stand resolute in the face of persecution. Is the church of today ready to take a stand for Jesus Christ even to the point of death? There are people today in other countries around the world who are dying gruesome deaths because of the gospel. They would rather die than to renounce Jesus Christ as their Savior and Lord. Will you? But you see the church then was going through its own share of persecutions; Christians and Jews in Rome were fleeing for their lives. The mentality of the Christians in Rome and the surrounding areas was different. Apparently, Paul had to reach back and walk them through the whole plan of salvation so they could be encouraged in the faith enough to survive. The church in Smyrna must have been strong in their faith. Jesus told them not to fear the sufferings to come but to endure. Their faith was stronger. We, as human beings, tend to do the things that we know are not right. Yet we do them anyway. Why? The draw and pull of sin toward our tainted, sinful nature.

The Beatitudes in Matthew Chapter 5 laid the basis for their foundation in the faith. These followers of Jesus Christ were ready to die for the faith. They lived the last two Beatitudes as Jesus stated;

Blessed are those who are persecuted for righteousness' sake,
For theirs is the kingdom of heaven.

"Blessed are you when they revile and persecute you, and say all kinds of evil against you falsely for My sake. Rejoice and be exceedingly glad, for great is your reward in heaven, for so they persecuted the prophets who were before you.
(Matthew 5:10-12)

Jesus told His disciples that they will be blessed if they do these things. But, He was not just telling them to do these things, going through the motions as most will do. Jesus was truthful with them and told the facts. They will be persecuted and they may die because of Him. He constantly reminded them throughout His ministry of His impending death and that they would suffer because of Him. Does this shed new light on our task at hand? I pray it does. He said that *when* you are persecuted rejoice and be glad. Why would anyone want to rejoice and be glad when they are being persecuted and possibly tortured, even killed? The next statement put it all in perspective. Jesus said "Great is your reward in heaven!" That is the greatest incentive you can receive, eternal reward in heaven. People in American churches have complacency that borders on lethargic. They would throw money at the problem, whether foreign or domestic, and not put hand to the plow regardless of the cost.

The pointed statement Jesus made to those in the Smyrnian church in Revelation 2:10 tells them exactly what is about to take place. He gives them a literal head up. So, these Christians know what is about to happen. He tells them in the beginning not to fear. He told them if they endure there will be a reward at the end. In the Matthew verses, it is the crown of life. The greatest of eternal rewards. The crown of life was given those who truly stood for the gospel and gave even their lives for the spreading of the gospel. Those who are martyred for the faith and endured to the end in the name of Jesus. The church in Smyrna was only one of two churches of the seven churches that did not receive a condemnation or correction given by Jesus.

SMYRNA: THE STEADFAST AND FAITHFUL

These things says the First and the Last, who was
dead, and came to life:
(Revelation 2:8)

Jesus begins His acknowledgement of the Smyrnian church by relating His own experiences, life and death, to what is about to happen to them. He tells them that this has happened to Me so be encouraged that I know what you are about to experience. His statement is one of encouragement and a source of strengthening. He was the first among the dead to be raised again to life and He will be the last and final word on life and death in the end. This sets the tone for those who are about to be as sheep led to the slaughter. As with all other churches in these two chapters in Revelation, there is a unique introduction of Himself. This introduction seems to highlight what is about to take place in the lives of those connected with that church. The people of the church in Smyrna were committed and obedient to the guidance of the Spirit of God. Does this give us a cause to pause for at least for a moment? Considering the notion that they followed through with obedience even to the death, how does this affect us in our belief today? Can we truly understand or even sympathize with their plight?

The beauty of all that is transpiring within this Body of Believers is that they have a grasp on faith and obedience I do not think we can fathom. Jesus knew their hearts and made the statement in that introductory verse to reassure and strengthen them in their motivation. Until this time, they had been faithful and steadfast in their dedication to the will of God. Now from this time forward they were probably more driven and focused than ever. Jesus is telling them ahead of time what is going to happen so they will prepare physically, but also that they will especially be prepared spiritually. He has assured them that He is going into battle with them and He is there regardless of the outcome. We do have the same assurance in our lives if we accept it and live it. The faithful followers at the church in Smyrna is a shining example of true obedience to the will of God, regardless of the cost.

SMYRNA: THE POOR BUT RICH

I know your works, tribulation, and poverty (but you are rich); and I know the blasphemy of those who say they are Jews and are not, but are a synagogue of Satan. (Revelation 2:9)

The church in ancient Smyrna was, by all accounts, humble in all their ways. This goes against the grain of the ideals of the city of Smyrna. The city was founded and grew out of pride, power, and wealth. The church was the true opposite of all that the city represented. Jesus knew that this church was going to face great persecution on all fronts because their stark contrast of ideals in comparison to those around them. It is ironic to note that Smyrna's high-end trade import and export item was myrrh. This was used for perfumes and particularly noted for its use in preparation of bodies for burial. Also, one of the three gifts of the Magi when they visited the child Jesus, was myrrh. The way we view the big picture should reflect on the relationship with the Lord. I do not believe that there are any coincidences in life, just Godly moments and opportunities. Jesus, in the way He told John concerning that church, knew that this church because of the faithfulness and strength would endure to the end. How can we use our knowledge of the Smyrnian church to learn and grow in faith?

The concern we have for the churches today are that they seem to believe the more they do the closer they are to right. No! By no means does this mean that our church is any better than the small church who struggles week to week. It is the measure of faith, not just surface faith, but soul binding faith. Remember, Jesus knows the heart. We may go through the motions on the surface and fool everybody around us. But, it is the Lord who sees. Who are we trying to serve, God or Mammon? Smyrna was a poor church in the world's eyes. But, they were rich in God's eyes because of their heart committed faith in Jesus Christ and His vision and mission for His church. Because of their humility, repentant heart, desire for the things of God, their mercy and peaceable spirit, and their meek approach to life in general, Jesus knew that they would be willing to stand strong without fear and stay the course to the end. Are we willing to finish the race strong in faith, regardless of the cost?

I know the blasphemy of those who say they are
Jews and are not, but are a synagogue of Satan.
(Revelation 2:9b)

As with any congregation of Believers, there are both good and those who are good but are easily swayed by the popular gossip and rumor. Do you recognize that within your congregation? Jesus condemned those who claim to be a Jew and yet are not. These were the ones probably held standing at one time in the Jewish belief system, but because of their faith in Jesus Christ, were not in the system anymore. They, most likely, are secret Christians and condemn those who are openly worshipping Jesus Christ. This is something they are unable to do. So, out of envy and professional jealousy, they make every effort to destroy the testimony of the congregation and those serving faithfully. These are probably the ones responsible for the persecution to come. Chances are this is how persecution will come into the modern church if we are not mindful. Jesus calls them out as the "synagogue of Satan." We are told by the Apostle Paul to test the spirits. This is true for everyone who comes into your presence, whether in the world, home, even in God's House.

Do not quench the Spirit. Do not despise proph-
ecies. Test all things; hold fast what is good.
Abstain from every form of evil.
(1 Thessalonians 5:19-22)

The Apostle John says concerning the testing of the spirits;

Beloved, do not believe every spirit, but test the
spirits, whether they are of God; because many
false prophets have gone out into the world.
(1 John 4:1)

The notion of the Spirit of God at work in the life of the Believer was a powerful belief until the early twentieth century. Though there remains some that follow this way of seeking God, the more power house movements of the nineteenth and twentieth have dwindled in their overall impact on the new society. The holiness movement in America made for a division in Christianity in general. The more traditional high church stayed the course, even in the twenty-first century, with reverent ritual ceremonies and grandiose facilities and massive cathedrals. The division is seen in those who seek a more spiritually minded approach. The holiness movement made its adverse attempt at the Pentecostal or charismatic approach to worship. There are others in the mix who add twists and turns to worshipping God. I am not saying that any of these are wrong, just different. The problem in the twenty-first century is that a whole new group of human has risen to the arena. The millennials have complicated the idea of worship. The traditional ritualistic worship sees it as a threat because they never did it like that so Jesus would not have done it like that. The Pentecostals are threatened because this group is threatening their claim on the Spirit and the gifts. Every new attempt at worship has cause great turmoil because every group thinks that their way is the right way. When in fact, they all are great in God's eyes. Jesus never told us the exact way to worship. He told us to love the Lord your God with all your heart, mind, soul, and strength, and love one another as He loved us.

Regardless to how you worship, it is irrelevant. It is who you worship that truly matters. The church at Smyrna knew that if they had the Spirit of God guiding and leading them in all their affairs, then was all good. Even though there were many in the church that tried and almost succeeded at destroying their testimony, they believed in the Lord Jesus Christ and knew without a doubt that He would strengthen them and deliver them in this life or the next. Now that's faith not fear. When you worship the Lord Jesus Christ, the Spirit of God or the Holy Spirit must be there or it is just another social gathering. Test all spirits that enter the doors of your congregation. I believe that even though the church at Smyrna was humble and separate from those in the world, they remained vigilant in their sensitivity to the Holy Spirit. This is how they remained faithful, even though persecution offered death. The Holy Spirit does not bring fear and death, but He brings peace and life. A church that is poor in spirit is one that grows into a church of mighty spiritual wealth in the Kingdom of God.

SMYRNA: THE OVERCOMERS

---

*He who has an ear, let him hear what the Spirit
says to the churches. He who overcomes shall not
be hurt by the second death.* (Revelation 2:11)

What can we take away from the church at Smyrna for use in today's church? I believe it is the simplicity of their faith. This is the strength and fearlessness of that faith. The church in Smyrna believed in the Beatitudes and they lived them out in their lives. They saw past the muck and sludge of everyday existence and saw the Holy Spirit leading and guiding them toward Jesus. The ones who sought Jesus in the power of the Holy Spirit in faith were the overcomers. Those who had faith in the world, prone to the spirit of the world or of the synagogue of Satan, were to be considered "up and comers." They cared more about how the world viewed and how Jesus saw them and their lack of faith. The overcomers were those who had ears that could hear what the Spirit says whereas the up and comers will probably never hear because of their deafness and lack of sensitivity to the word of God.

HOW FAR ARE WE OFF TARGET?

The desire to be closer to Jesus Christ in a real intimate relationship with Him should be our priority. We should seek first the Kingdom of God and all His righteousness and then all things will be added to us. This was the hope lived out by those at the church in the city of Smyrna and should be an example to us even today. Now for those who were of the synagogue of Satan? Well, by the way Jesus spoke concerning them, we know their fate. There was no reason that they also could receive redemption and grace through the Holy Spirit. They needed to seek first the Holy Spirit to guide and lead them away from those things which led them astray. The church today is no different. The beauty of this prophesy is that it gives us an understanding and a knowledge that the people of the Smyrna church did not have to their advantage. But, just as they had the Spirit of God as a guide and leader for their faith, so we do as well. There remains a great opportunity for the church which is not so far down the rabbit hole that there is no hope. The light that we see at the end of that tunnel of life is our hope and that hope rests in faith in the Lord Jesus Christ through power of the Holy Spirit.

TEACHING MOMENTS FROM THE CHURCH IN SMYRNA

1. What do you think was the greatest strength the church in Smyrna had shown as an example?

2. What do you think is meant by the fact that a majority of the church members in Smyrna were poor but rich? How does this effect your understanding of the church and its role in the plans of God?

3. The church in Smyrna was severely persecuted for their faith, how does this reflect on your understanding of faith and its strength in the growth of the Body of Christ in the world?

4. Those who called themselves Christian but played crucial roles in the destruction of congregations, who are they in your congregation? How can your church be the church that is poor but rich in spirit?

Closing Prayer:

Heavenly Father, Gracious Lord, cleanse my heart from the discouragement found within the world. Lord, help me seek your ways through the power of the Holy Spirit. May I seek first Your Kingdom and all Your righteousness to be fully focused on Your will and Yours alone. In Jesus' Name, Amen.

CHAPTER 3

PERGAMOS: THE DECEITFUL COMPROMISE

*I know your works, and where you dwell, where
Satan's throne is.* (Revelation 2:13a)

*But I have a few things against you, because
you have there those who hold the doctrine of
Balaam, who taught Balak to put a stumbling
block before the children of Israel, to eat things
sacrificed to idols, and to commit sexual immorality.* (Revelation 2:14)

The church at Pergamos was one of deceit and compromise
in the eyes of the Lord. The faithfulness of the few apparently did
not outweigh that of the many. They seemed to hold fast to the
ways of the Lord but they were easily swayed from the truth. The
most bold statement here is that He is calling their dwelling place
the throne of Satan. This says much about their relationship to the
things of the world. Despite those among them who stand firm
against the enemy, there are more who are just as easily influenced
by the wiles of the devil.

The Lord mentions the fact that this church holds to the doctrine of Balaam. This seems to point to his presumptuous attitude
and personality. Despite God's counsel to not go to Balak, Balaam
remained unmoved in his heart. Even though he sent the first group
of diviners away, he was hesitant. His heart was seeking the honor
of a king. The second group that was sent, larger than the first was
sent to show his importance to the king of Moab. This appealed to

his pride and desire for power. At this, he prepared himself for the journey, even before the Lord spoke to him. He assumed the Lord was blessing the journey when in fact the Lord gave him a condition to follow before He would bless the journey. He told Balaam if the men would call him out to go with them, then he would. But, he was only to do what the Lord told him. True to form, Balaam only seemed to hear half of what the Lord told him. He had his mind made we he rose the next morning. The men did not call on him. He rose on his own accord and went to them. Because of this act of defiance on the part of Balaam, the Lord sent the angel of the Lord to destroy him.

How many times have we been stubborn in our ways and ventured out on our own, despite what God has given us? When Balaam set out with the assumption that God was going to bless him and his journey, he set in motion a series of events that placed a huge stumbling block before the people of Israel. God allowed him to continue as he repented. But, he was still given the word from the Lord that he only speaks what God tells him.

The interesting part of this and its relation to the connection in the New Testament, even from Jesus' beginnings in His ministry, it recalls those times during the temptations of Jesus by Satan. Remember, in the Balaam saga, Balak brings Balaam to three vantage points from where he gave Balaam a clear view of the armies of Israel and each time he give an offer and each time Balaam refuses him. The problem here seems to be that Balaam even listened to Balak and that he followed to these mountain tops gave the notion that he was considering the offers. Balaam, even though he seemed to be one who sought God's counsel, it was more that he was going through the motions and had no intention carrying out what the Lord God instructed him. In the end, all that Balaam did in the eyes of the Lord was lead the people down the wrong path, not as much by his words but by his actions.

The story of Balaam is one that needs to be considered in more detail, but not now. The difference between him, before his enemies, and the temptation of Jesus in the wilderness was the heart and focus of Balaam was on what he could press to gain from Balak. Jesus' heart was on the things of above and He sought only what the Father's counsel in all things. The difference is clear and evident in what Jesus was telling John in the revelation for Pergamos. Jesus was warning the church at Pergamos to not fall into the same trap and snare of Satan as Balaam.

Another reason for the city of Pergamos to be considered as the "throne of Satan," it had three known worship centers within the city itself. Their culture revolved around these three temples. One was dedicated to the Roman emperor, the next was dedicated to the goddess Athena and the third dedicated to Zeus, the king of the Greek gods on Olympus. These were considered the three rulers of their society. The representation of the various cultural influences established the city of Pergamos the cultural and religious center of Asia Minor. Even though the previous cities mentioned were religious centers as well, they did not compare to the power represented in Pergamos. These three pagan temples were frequented by the people and therefore they even became influences in the church as well.

Anytime there are strong cultural authorities at work in a society, there is compromise. This is the concern with the church today. As much as we do not want to admit it, the culture in America has dictated much within the church culturally. Any choices whether in the church or even in the lives of individual members, it is more than just surface belief. The faith must come from the heart. Balaam was a Believer, but only to his benefit. Where do we stand when it comes to total obedience to the Lord Jesus through the guidance of the Holy Spirit? Do we allow Satan to deceive us and guide our hearts down a path of destruction or do we look to the Lord from our hearts and follow Him alone in total obedience to Him?

Thus you also have those who hold the doctrine of
the Nicolaitans, which thing I hate.
(Revelation 2:15)

The concern of the Lord Jesus, regarding those who were the so-called Nicolaitans, was that they held to the same beliefs as the way of Balaam. Everything the Jerusalem Council in Acts 15 established in terms of the practices of Gentile Christians was set for the benefit of everybody. But, primarily, the Jerusalem Council set standards for the Gentiles to follow so that they would not stumble or cause others to stumble in their beliefs. The not eating of food sacrificed to idols and the drinking of blood were dietary concerns that, during the day, would cause those who participated to fall back into that way of pagan belief and life style. The third was to refrain from sexual immorality. This was a given because it was an abomination, but also because it was practiced in the temples during worship, it became of great concern for the church. The church was made up of converts from the pagan world and, with any people that engrained in their culture, it takes a certain amount mentoring and empowering to direct them away from the influences of their past. How do we learn from the church in Pergamos? How do take what we learn from them and apply it to our own church?

PERGAMOS: THE FEW AND THE FAITHFUL

---

*And you hold fast to My name, and did not deny
My faith even in the days in which Antipas was
My faithful martyr, who was killed among you,
where Satan dwells.* (Revelation 2:13b)

In the church, even when most the people were falling into Satan's traps, a remnant remained, held strong in the faith and focused on the task at hand, including martyrdom. It takes a strong resolve and unwavering faith to stand firm in times of great persecution. Antipas, according to Jesus in this passage, was truly faithful even to death. Tradition tells that Antipas was taken by those in the city and put in a brass bowl and roasted alive because of his faith. If the others in the church were witnesses to this horrific act, then chances are that this was the occasion of their lack motivation to serve God. Fear is a great motivator in times of great persecution and this was during the time of the Emperor Vespasian, who was among the worst in terms of torture. Vespasian hated the Christians and relished at the opportunity to torture and kill as many as possible. When all is considered, the remnant of the church most have exhibited a focus and a pure heart before the Lord. With the influence of those within the church and the pressure from outside, Jesus acknowledged the fact that the remnant was truly faithful in walk with Him.

Blessed are the pure in heart, for they shall see God. (Matthew 5:8)

This verse demonstrates the focus of the walk of those among the people who ignored the world and even the ones who influenced peers within the church. This group of Believers brings to remembrance a recall of the cities of Sodom and Gomorrah. When the angels of the Lord came down, Abraham begged them concerning those in the city. He pleaded with them that if there were fifty righteous people that the city would be spared. Abraham debated down to the point of ten righteous people that they would spare the city. Well, the story gives the impression that there were none except for Lot and his family and only they were spared from the wrath of God. I believe that this is the case with not only the church in Pergamos but the other churches who needed to repent.

Jesus set the standard for the righteous who can stand before a Holy God. A person must be pure in heart. God is righteous and jealous. He cannot look upon sin, and therefore the person who wants to be in eternity with Him must be pure in heart. Despite the conditions of those around you, there must be consistency in your walk with Him. The one who is pure in heart is one who also is living all the previous Beatitudes. The walk with God should be one of pure focus and love for Him. There was a remnant of people who apparently witnessed the martyrdom of one of their own, Antipas. This influenced the church. Jesus mentioned this incident to press a point for the people. Apparently, the martyr of Antipas was particularly gruesome and had an enduring impact on the church. Many fell away, but those who were strong in the Lord and pure in their focus, stayed the course. It was only through the power and guidance of the Holy Spirit that these few and faithful could stand firm.

PERGAMOS: THE FINAL CALL

Repent, or else I will come to you quickly and will fight against them with the sword of My mouth. (Revelation 2:16)

Jesus calls, as He does to all the churches, the people to repentance. Despite all their sin, Jesus has given them the opportunity to turn back to Him. He tells them pointedly what they must do to be in a right relationship. There are no gray areas when Jesus tells you to repent. When He gives the church a chance to repent, it is an imperative. Even though He has unconditional love for the people, He knows the heart. The present day church is not immune to the call to repentance. If anything, the call is more urgent. In the case of the church at Pergamos, He shows the urgency by stating one word "repent." This not different when He issued the great commission in Matthew Chapter 28. He commands His people to "Go." Because this command has already been issued, the one word command to repent is even more powerful. The condition or consequence of not following through with the command is immediate wrath. The implication is that by now we should know better and therefore it would be highly advisable to follow the directive. Also, we can see the ways and means of the congregation as seeing their worship of Christ as secondary to their everyday lives.

The notion introduced here even more intently than the others so far is that they are compromising the faith for a more pleasurable life. Jesus never promised that our lives would be easier as Christians. He told the disciples and us that life would be more difficult and that we would truly be persecuted. The persecution is not physical for everybody, but He did say that we would be hated for His name's sake. The world hated Him, so why would the world not hate us as well because we are His and represent Him? In Jesus' directive to repent, there are no gray areas to interpret so why do we have to seek out scholars and experts on the subject? The reason that the Christian sees the need to search out the opinion of those more scholarly than themselves is to affirm their own assumptions. Therefore, establishing the broader spectrum of their understanding and rationalizing their own misinterpretation of Scripture. Look at what Jesus says: He will come quickly and fight against them with the sword of His mouth. This is devastating, eternally, because you need to keep in mind that the sword of His mouth is the double-edged sword which is the Word of God. This sword is what defeated Satan at the temptation of Jesus in the wilderness. How much more do you consider yourself than Satan at defeating the Word of God? I did not think so!

PERGAMOS: THE REWARD, A SOLID FOUNDATION

To him who overcomes I will give some of the hidden manna to eat. And I will give him a white stone, and on the stone a new name written which no one knows except him who receives it.
(Revelation 2:17)

There are a few rewards that are to be given to those who persevere to the end and stay the course. The first reward comes in the form of the very substance that maintained the children of Israel while they wandered in the wilderness for forty years. This may not have meant much to the Gentile Christians, but to the Jewish Christians of that church, it would point to God's personal care for those whom He loves. But, the Gentile Christians would have been schooled in the historical significance and therefore it would have been recognized more spiritual and not physical. The manna would have also been that which was hidden from anyone other than the Jewish people who were called out by God and led from Egypt through the wilderness.

Blessed are those who hunger and thirst
for righteousness,
For they shall be filled.
(Matthew 5:6)

The manna which is hidden is found in the righteousness of the Son of God. Jesus was teaching the disciples that the greatest sustenance is found in the righteousness of God. He sought God's counsel and His righteousness in everything He said or the work done. The glory was for the Father, not even for the Son, as He walk among us. As we hunger and thirst after the righteousness of God, do we truly know for what we are seeking? It should be our greatest desire in life to seek after the righteousness of God. The congregation of Believers are to be fervent in their pursuit of this righteousness because it will be the only thing that will sustain the true Christian in their faith and life. Apart from the guidance and power of the Holy Spirit, our fruitless attempts at achieving the righteousness of God will lead us down a path of despair. Because the Son is the Glory of the Father, then it follows that the Spirit is the one to which the true follower of Jesus Christ should rely and follow.

The second of the rewards presented to the church is that of a white stone. The stone is the sign of stability and that which establishes the foundation onto which the building of the church should stand. The color white gives the understanding of purity and unity. The church needs to be set its foundations in the Lord. The stone is set as a representation of a solid and firm faith that cannot be moved regardless of the storms.

Whoever comes to Me, and hears My sayings and does them, I will show you whom he is like: He is like a man building a house, who dug deep and laid the foundation on the rock. And when the flood arose, the stream beat vehemently against that house, and could not shake it, for it was founded on the rock. (Luke 6:47-48)

This parable speaks concerning the one who does not just one thing but all three to establish the firm and steady foundation in the faith. They are needed to receive the reward prepared for those whom the Lord loves. First, He says "whoever *comes* to Me." This statement infers that all have access to Him and all are called unto Him. So, we must realize that it is an open invitation to mercy, grace and faith in Jesus Christ. The life in Christ is one that affirms our stability and confirms our relationship with Him. The fact Jesus said that the man building the house, dug deep and laid the foundation on rock, assumes that it is not something given without some hard effort of our own. The church at Pergamos seemed to waver from the faith in fear because of the least bit of effort. They did not want to work out their salvation with fear and trembling. The church wanted to take the easy path and that is what led to their compromising mentality. The house built on the rock, because the builder dug deep into the earth until he found rock, the footings for the house added to its stability and thus the larger the house. It is no different with the church. The deeper and more solid the foundation, the more stable the church in their faith.

The second condition set by Jesus in the parable is that the individual must also *hear* His words. What a concept! Most of the time, as we conduct our lives, we hear only what we want to hear. Most people hear only what benefits them. The people in the churches are no different in their mentality. The human ideal for their life is to speak first and then maybe listen. The idea is to just speak. I was told growing up that if you are a talker then you are generally not a good listener. This is because when one's mouth is moving then the ears are disengaged. In like manner, when one's mouth is closed then the ears are opened. I don't know the truth of this, physiologically, but it makes perfect sense. I have known those, and I am among them at times, who have lengthy prayers that tend to babble. Then, they expect God to answer because they have spoken so much. But, the problem may be that *He* cannot get a word in edge ways. The Lord Jesus explains to His disciples in the parable of the sower and the hearers of the word.

> *Now he who received seed among the thorns is he*
> *who hears the word, and the cares of this world*
> *and the deceitfulness of riches choke the word,*
> *and he becomes unfruitful.* (Matthew 13:22)

The ones who received seed among the thorns are the church in Pergamos because they are influenced by the world and all those around them. As He said in the explanation, the cares of the world and the deceitfulness of riches choke out the word. The church in Pergamos was one that heard the word of God preached but they were easily distracted. This led to the compromising spirit among the Believers. The Psalmist says that we hear the voice of the Lord:

> *The voice of the* Lord *is over the waters;*
> *The God of glory thunders;*
> *The* Lord *is over many waters.*
> *The voice of the* Lord *is powerful;*
> *The voice of the* Lord *is full of majesty.*
> (Psalm 29:3-4)

Those who seek the Lord will hear His voice calling out to them. The voice of the Lord is clearly recognizable to those who know His voice. The beauty of God the Father, Son and the Holy Spirit is they speak not just to our ears but to our soul and spirit. As His sheep, we will know His voice and will follow His call.

But he who heard and did nothing is like a man who built a house on the earth without a foundation, against which the stream beat vehe-mently; and immediately it fell. And the ruin of that house was great. (Luke 6:49)

Jesus goes on to say in the parable of the house on the foundation that the one who heard and did nothing is like the man who builds the house on the earth with no foundation. For the most part, most churches have this sort of foundation in their congregation. The world comes against the house and without the firm foundation, there is nothing to hold it firm. The house will fall. Those in the church who listen and absorb the Word but do not put it to action has no purpose. It will fall. It is not like they do not know what to do. They choose to sit in the pew and listen. Most of the time, these same people are those who have opinions and suggestions on everything pertaining the health and growth of the church. This is what is wrong with the church today! We need to listen to the voice of God and seek His vision for growth in our churches. I have always told my congregation that I would rather have ten people who were totally surrendered and committed to the Word and work of Christ rather than two-hundred who merely warm the pews.

The final point that Jesus brought out was that we need to be *doers* of the Word and not just hearers. This is what settles the footings of the foundation solid in its place. You must put the Word of God in action and share it with others. In the Letter of James, he makes a pointed argument that we must not only be hearers of the word we must put action to the Word of God.

But be doers of the word, and not hearers only, deceiving yourselves. For if anyone is a hearer of the word and not a doer, he is like a man observing his natural face in a mirror; for he observes himself, goes away, and immediately forgets what kind of man he was. But he who looks into the perfect law of liberty and continues in it, and is not a forgetful hearer but a doer of the work, this one will be blessed in what he does.
(James 1:22-25)

The Word of God is to be given away and thus we need to not only be hearers, but doers of the Word. The church in Pergamos seemed to possess a lethargic attitude toward putting the Word into action. Much of this, like many church people today, believe that action is the extra mile which you should do but you are not required to do. When Jesus tells His disciples that if someone tells you to go with them a mile, you go the second mile. If someone takes your cloak, then give them your tunic as well. The point is that there should be considered a second mile for a person who serves in ministry. The second mile is every mile, every moment of everyday.

James tells the reader that the one who hears the Word only, and is not a doer of the Word, is like a man who observes himself in a mirror. He says that the man observes himself, goes away, and immediately forgets. He forgets because he is distracted by everything else around and any influences. He loses the personal understanding of his own life. You cannot hear the Word without sharing the Word of God. He continues to say that if you are not a forgetful hearer, but one who is a doer of the work per His Word, then you will be blessed in what you do. Jesus encouraged His followers, especially those disciples He chose, that if they believe in Him to not only hear what He said to them, but put it into action. He demonstrated for them the way to action. Jesus was the ultimate teacher. He put His disciples into real world circumstances and showed them how to resolve the issues. In other words, they could not just listen to Jesus and walk away without putting their hand to the plow and live the Word. The reality of it is that the church in Pergamos was one of hearers and not doers of the Word. Therefore, they did not understand fully the importance that the Word into action played in their salvation. Considering the words of Jesus to John in Revelation 2:17, the reward was great for those in the church in Pergamos who would just repent and not only be hearers but doers of the Word. Those people who did these things would not only have their foundation upon the pure white rock of Jesus Christ. But, they would be given a special name that identifies and ties them to God that only they would know. What a beautiful and marvelous picture for eternity!

HOW FAR ARE WE OFF TARGET?

He who has an ear, let him hear what the Spirit says to the churches. To him who overcomes I will give some of the hidden manna to eat. And I will give him a white stone, and on the stone a new name written which no one knows except him who receives it. (Revelation 2:17)

The call of Jesus to repent is one that echoes throughout the ages. If you are a Believer in Jesus and follow all His commandments and statutes, we know that the Holy Spirit leads and guides us into all righteousness. Just because you say that you are a Christian does not mean you *are* a Christian. Because you go to church does not make you a Christian. If you do all the good deeds available for you to accomplish, this does not mean that you will go to heaven for eternity. The road to hell is paved with good works and good intentions. The good news is that Jesus has given us the opportunity and the Spirit to guide us onto the right path in His Will. The church today is filled with people who are under the impression that because they were born into generations of Christians or they knelt at the altar once that is all that is required. This is the true deception! Test the spirits that cross your paths whether in your life, in your home and your church. Yes, in your church, there are those who can lead you down the wrong path! The Word of God is Truth and that truth and no other can set you free! Consider the church in Pergamos and how far off the reservation they traveled because of fear. Live in the Spirit of Jesus Christ! His Holy Spirit! He will guide you down the right path in the power and authority of the Holy Spirit.

TEACHING MOMENTS FROM PERGAMOS

1. As we look at the church today, how can we improve on the relationship we have in the community?

2. Are you compromising the teachings of Christ for tradition?

3. There are some great sounding doctrines out there in the world. How is your church responding to the Gospel? Are you compromising and following the deceitfulness of the ways of the world or are you standing strong and firm on the gospel of Jesus Christ?

Let us Pray;

Heavenly Father, be with me in all my unworthiness and light the path before me. Cleanse my heart, Lord. Put a right spirit within me, Lord, that I may not only be a hearer but a doer of the Word. May I glorify you all that I say and do in accordance to Your Will. In Jesus' Name, Amen.

CHAPTER 4

THE CHURCH IN THYATIRA: JEZEBEL'S HOUSE

Nevertheless I have a few things against you, because you allow that woman Jezebel, who calls herself a prophetess, to teach and seduce My servants to commit sexual immorality and eat things sacrificed to idols. And I gave her time to repent of her sexual immorality, and she did not repent. (Revelation 2:20-21)

The church in Thyatira is one that will make the Christian in the pew and those with questionable faith take notice of their relationship with Christ. The congregation is one who is taken by an individual. In many churches today, some people are focused on the pastor and not on the message and Christ. Jesus wants to be the focal point of our love and faithfulness. In the church in Thyatira there must have been a woman of great influence not only in the church but in the community. The history of the city is sparse at best. The chief commerce was linens and primarily noted for the processing of fine purple linens. If you notice as the seven churches begin to reveal their stories, this church seems to be tied to a person of great influence. Jesus seems to place blame for the misdirection of the church on an individual, but I propose the idea of a group of influential people.

The city and the church, historically, are the smallest in comparison to the other cities and churches mentioned in Revelation. Yet, more time and space is committed to Jesus' concern for this church than any other. The one thing that churches today do not discern as to anything else and that is teachings and doctrine circulated, taught, and preached in the church. Apparently, this was a great concern for Jesus and the church in Thyatira. He was unyielding in His focus on those with false teachings. Many letters in the New Testament have major portions dedicated to recognizing and ridding themselves of false teachers. Jesus considered the religious leaders of His day as false teachers because they claimed superiority of the law and the prophets yet they did not know it.

The Jezebel, a name given to the person or persons leading the saints away, has spread teachings that are contrary to basic teachings set in place by Jesus Himself. This person was empowering and spoke with authority. The authority was obviously not of God, but the people were following the teachings and influence anyway. There is no record of the beginnings of this church, but it is thought to be one that came from Paul's teachings in Ephesus or maybe even as late as John's preaching in Smyrna. Nevertheless, the Jezebel mentioned is a part of the faction that has been trying to destroy the church from the start. If you recall, the mentality of Queen Jezebel, the wife of Ahab, was evil. She was power hungry and would kill anyone who would stand in the way without regard for anyone or anything.

Then Jezebel his wife said to him, "You now exercise authority over Israel! Arise, eat food, and let your heart be cheerful; I will give you the vineyard of Naboth the Jezreelite."

And she wrote letters in Ahab's name, sealed them with his seal, and sent the letters to the elders and the nobles who were dwelling in the city with Naboth.
(1 Kings 21:7-8)

The deceitfulness of Jezebel knew no bounds and no one was going to stand in the way of her power and glory. Ahab was her stepping stone. She was from Sidon, the daughter of the king. If she was to take over the throne of Israel, then she could be more powerful than all among the kings of the region. Jezebel's sights were set higher than Ahab. He was merely a tool. Her manipulation of Ahab made her the most dangerous person to the throne and for God's relationship to His people.

The idea of manipulation, as it relates to the church in Thyatira, is at the core of why Jesus was so concerned for the people and that He was focused on this one person or group of people. Today, the churches are led astray by complacency and tolerance in modern society. If you do not accept the professions and norms of the society, then laws are created to force you into compliance. Therefore, it is so important to test and follow the truth of Jesus and some teaching that makes you feel good. Chances are the message is false. The biggest concern of Jesus in the Revelation passage is that the church is being fooled into believing a false doctrine that seems right and good and they do not know the difference. This speaks to the possible immaturity of those within the congregation.

THYATIRA: PURIFICATION AND DELIVERANCE

"And to the angel of the church in Thyatira
write,

'These things says the Son of God, who has eyes
like a flame of fire, and His feet like fine brass:
(Revelation 2:18)

The vision of Jesus as the Son of God is given in utter power and authority. His eyes are as flames of fire. Fire in the Scriptures denotes power. The reinforcement of the mention that He is the Son of God. This shows from whom and by whom His comes. The beauty of the scene is in power and love. God's love and mercy is everlasting and never ends. The eternal flames seen in His eyes gives those in the church the true sense of His authority and power over the one called Jezebel. How many Jezebels are in churches today? The world does not see them for who they are, but Jesus knows the heart and mind of those He loves. Fire is associated with refining to the point of purity. Like gold, the more it is refined in the fire, the more purified it becomes. So, it is with our relationship with the Lord. The flames of fire in the eyes of the Lord Jesus see the depths of the heart and soul. In seeing these things, He can also refine and purify the soul through the power and work of the Holy Spirit. Jesus wants the church to see that they can only be delivered and then purified through Him.

The church today is no different in that it must turn back to Him and away from the worldly influences that dictate what they should believe. As churches become more tolerant in their beliefs, they also justify their actions because they say Jesus told us to love them. This does not mean to agree with them and change our doctrine because of them! He said to love the sinner but hate the sin. The problem occurs when we tend to accept them to the point of rationalization and excuses in the name of the love of God. Wars were fought over the centuries in the name of God. Much blood was shed in the name of Jesus, but Jesus said that many will come in His name and cry "Lord, Lord!" and He will say, "Depart from me for I never knew you." How many of us look to leaders in the world, or even in the pulpit, not knowing that they are leading many astray? The eyes of the Son of God, as flames of fire, are looking now into the heart of the church even today! What is He seeing in the heart of your church?

The feet, as those of fine brass, seem to refer to the authority and steadfastness of the gospel of Christ. Jesus stands firm and steady on the Word of God and its authority. He is the fulfilment of the law and all that it stands for is Truth. Today, in the United States, they have been making laws to remove The Ten Commandments from schools and court houses. Also, prayer is being removed from the schools and courts. The legalization of same-sex marriages in the United States would have been scoffed at by authorities, especially the church. Today, mainline denominations have gay and lesbian pastors, teachers, bishops, and major authority figures in the churches. Power and authority has been ripped from the hands of the churches and put into the hands of the few. Has the church followed Jezebel so far down the rabbit hole that we cannot climb our way out? The Holy Spirit has been set outside the doors and replaced by the spirit of the world and the wiles of Satan. Jezebel's sole purpose was to obtain full power and authority, but Jesus stands before the church ready to deliver and purify. He wants to place authority once again into the hands of the church, but only with the Holy Spirit's authority.

THYATIRA: SERVICE BASED ON LOVE, FAITH AND PATIENCE

I know your works, love, service, faith, and your patience; and as for your works, the last are more than the first. (Revelation 2:19)

The Lord knows your heart and mind. He sees that there are those who are progressing in the faith as it is with every church. The people within a given congregation are diverse and unique. The beauty of each congregation is found in their diversity and, in many cases in the world's eyes, there lies their weakness. The exploitation of one or the other is seen in our responses. The world brings great appeal to the pleasures of life, but with that appeal is also the evil therein. Jesus is telling the church that He knows them and their works. The works that we go out of our way to do for others is the strength. The defense He is making for those who are faithful is that in the works is love, faith and patience. The focus and motivation of those in a congregation is what drives them in their faith.

Love should be the cornerstone of the whole faith of the Body of Believers. The love for Jesus Christ must be first and foremost. The Lord Jesus gave His disciples two basic commands that needed to be followed. The first is to love the Lord your God with all your heart, mind, soul and strength. The next is just as important and that is to love one another as He has loved us. The former, for obvious reasons, serves as precedent to the latter. The most important point is that we cannot love one another if we do not love the Lord God. The love for one another naturally flows from the love of God. The love of God brings both power and validity to loving one another. We cannot do this on our own. There must be an intervention of the Holy Spirit with the broken and humbled; and with the poor in spirit of our own for the molding of the two to take place. This was evident in the church in Thyatira. The church was dealing with internal and external corruption. It took a toll on the faithful among the congregation. The love of God in Jesus Christ through the power of the Holy Spirit must be the source of strength and focus for not only this Body of Believers but for today's church.

The center and foundation of all that belongs to Christ is centered in love. But, love is built and grows out of faith. It is true that without love, faith is nothing. The Apostle Paul tells the Corinthian church that love is at the heart of everything. Apart from love, life is meaningless and considered nothing.

Though I speak with the tongues of men and of angels, but have not love, I have become sounding brass or a clanging cymbal. And though I have the gift of prophecy, and understand all mysteries and all knowledge, and though I have all faith, so that I could remove mountains, but have not love, I am nothing.
(1 Corinthians 13:1-2)

The key to understanding the beauty of the universe is found in love. The natural outflow of the unconditional love that comes from a relationship with Jesus Christ is faith. The 1 Corinthians passage in Chapter 13 is focused solely on love. But, from that love comes the faith that helps the individual grow into a closer relationship with Christ. The writer of Hebrews gives the best definition concerning a true understanding of faith:

Now faith is the substance of things hoped for,
the evidence of things not seen. (Hebrews 11:1)

Faith is not true faith apart from love. The church in Thyatira, being a corrupt church from all influences, was directed by the choices they made in accordance to their faith. This made the difference in how they responded to controversy and persecution. They looked to the other churches in the region for assistance and strength. The guidance and authority that the church in Thyatira with those in the city was the basis for the corrupt nature of their ways. They relied on the approval and direction from those in authority outside of the church. The work of the Holy Spirit expressed in the congregation through manifestations found in the ever-growing love and faith of the people of God. The church in Thyatira was failing many things together because did not rely on the Holy Spirit, but relied on the flesh and corrupted by the ways of the world.

There were those within the Believers who sought direction from the Holy Spirit. This meant that there were many in leadership positions that merely sought after peer political acceptance. Because of the worldly influences at work in the church, Jesus saw that there also were those among the Believers who were patient and strong in the faith. The basis for which the Lord had set a standard for the survival of the church.

Now a certain woman named Lydia heard us.
She was a seller of purple from the city of Thyat-
ira, who worshiped God. The Lord opened her
heart to heed the things spoken by Paul. And
when she and her household were baptized, she
begged us, saying, "If you have judged me to be
faithful to the Lord, come to my house and stay."
So she persuaded us. (Acts 16:14-15)

The few times that Thyatira is mentioned in Scripture is found in the Acts of the Apostles. In this passage, we learn of a woman named Lydia. She seemed to be a lover of God and she was a merchant as well. The enterprising nature of her business gives the impression of the mentality of those in the region concerning women and their status. Lydia was one who, per Acts 16, bought and sold fine purple linen. She was a prosperous business woman. This is interesting because the ancient world was looked upon as a male dominated society. This gives us eyes into the cultural ideals and business practices of the ancient world of Asia Minor. Even though the city of Thyatira was considered the smallest of the seven churches in Revelation, the buying and selling of fine linen was a very lucrative one. Lydia apparently had a home in Philippi too. The Scripture says that she persuaded them to come stay with her.

Paul and Silas, upon entering Philippi, went down to the river to pray. This was the common practice of the day. Luke said, in verse thirteen, that on the Sabbath day they went down to the river to pray because this was the practice. It must have been a solitary place. If it was common practice, then it must have been a serene environment. When they got there, they saw some women praying and began speaking with them concerning the Lord Jesus Christ. Lydia wasn't part of the group but she overheard them speaking with the other women. Maybe she was separate because she was a part of another class because of her status as a merchant, who knows. The point is that she heard Paul and the others speaking concerning Jesus and she responded. Lydia was from Thyatira and she had dealings with people regularly in Philippi because she had a home there. We do not see whether the other women responded to the call of Christ. But, we do know that Lydia and all her household responded and was baptized in the name of Jesus.

---

*So they went out of the prison and entered the
house of Lydia; and when they had seen the
brethren, they encouraged them and departed.*
(Acts 16:40)

Following their release from prison, Paul, Silas and the rest of the entourage went to Lydia's home and encouraged the Believers. Then, they departed the city of Philippi and went to Thessalonica. He considered Lydia and her household a kindred spirit and one who loved the Lord so he trusted her. The understanding here could be implied that because the point was made that she was from Thyatira gave way to the idea of the church. This is because she could have been responsible for the establishment of the church later in that city. This is speculation, but the possibility is there and establishes the mentality of the people of the church at the time of the revelation. If this church was established by a wealthy merchant and business woman, then it could be that the church consisted of those who were from the same circles of influence. This is true speculation, but look at the Lord's concern for the church. He saw the church, even though they were faithful in many ways, they lacked self-control when it came to the influences of the world. This implies a middle to upper class influence based on the notion of wealth and power.

THYATIRA: JEZEBEL IS THE PATH TO DESTRUCTION

Indeed I will cast her into a sickbed, and those
who commit adultery with her into great
tribulation, unless they repent of their deeds.
(Revelation 2:22)

Jesus tells His people to turn away from that which leads you astray. The world, the Jezebel, is the harlot of evil that draws the faithful into a false sense of hope. Then, once you realize how far you have wandered off the way, it is too late. The moral compass of the church today is spinning out of control and needs to be set true again. The church must allow the Holy Spirit to work and have authority over the enemy. He tells us here that there remains hope, but it can only be found through repentance. The open door for those who repent is an example of God's mercy and grace. He does not have to give them any opportunity to repent, but in His glorious mercy He does not want anyone to die in their sins.

I will kill her children with death, and all the
churches shall know that I am He who searches
the minds and hearts. And I will give to each one
of you according to your works.
(Revelation 2:23)

The opportunity of repentance is available for those who choose to accept Jesus Christ as savior and follow Him in all their ways. Lydia chose to follow Jesus and share that belief with others. If she carried this knowledge and love for Christ back to Thyatira, we are not sure. The beauty of the story is that she loved God and she grew in that love upon learning of the love of Jesus Christ His Son. This had to be a great revelation for her and her family. Jesus said that He would kill all the children of deception that were part of the Jezebel. All those who were taken in by the charms of the world. He says that He would make an example of them. I, for one, would not want Jesus to make an example of me. The problem of people in the world today is that they do not realize that He is the one who searches the minds and hearts. This should be a sobering fact to all people especially to those who believe. But, He says that He will make an example for all nations to know that He is the Lord and that He is the only one who judges the hearts and minds of individuals. Are you willing to take the chance that God is not concerned with the skeletons in your closet?

THYATIRA: THOSE FAITHFUL IN THE HOUSEHOLD OF GOD

Now to you I say, and to the rest in Thyatira, as many as do not have this doctrine, who have not known the depths of Satan, as they say, I will put on you no other burden. But hold fast what you have till I come. And he who overcomes, and keeps My works until the end, to him I will give power over the nations—

*'He shall rule them with a rod of iron;
They shall be dashed to pieces like the potter's vessels' —*

as I also have received from My Father; and I will give him the morning star.
(Revelation 2:24-28)

The Lord is offering protection to those who do not hold to the doctrine offered by the world. The faith of the ones not only in the church but also in the city itself shows that Christ was not through with the people. He continues to work for the church to completion in the city of Thyatira. This was the mission of those in that church.

The same call as in the church today. He tells us that we are to be in the world but we are not of the world. The one who stays faithful and serves in obedience to His word, then they will receive rewards. He will not burden them with more burdens but will give them power over all the nations. Those who were in power and are humble servants of Jesus Christ, will be rewarded greatly. The first shall be last and the last shall be first.

HOW FAR ARE WE OFF TARGET?

He who has an ear, let him hear what the Spirit
says to the churches.
(Revelation 2:29)

The concern I have for the church today rests in the idea of tolerance. The churches today, for the most part, work off the premise that we should love the sinner despite the sin. Twenty years ago, the idea was that we needed to love the sinner and hate the sin. How far are we off target? Today we cannot see the target for the trees. The reason for this is seen in the focus of the church on those sinners. Before those same sinners were counseled and led to repentance. Today they are accepted and made pastors and bishops. As the forests of sin has grown and has not been thinned out and cut back, we cannot see clearly the mission that has been given to us because we choose to accept the sin and tolerate the worldly abominations of the world.

Can we ever turn back and get right with the Lord? Yes, absolutely! If the church begins to turn back to the guidance of the Holy Spirit, then the Spirit will be able to clear the forests of sin and the mission and target will be made clear once again. Trust in Him in all you do and He will guide your paths. He will make your way straight. There is always a way of repentance. But, He will also give them over to their ways and lusts. Open your hearts to the Spirit of Christ and He will lead you down the paths of righteousness for His name's sake. The opportunities He makes for those who love Him will lead them to more authority and power than one could imagine. Glory to God in the Highest and to His Son Jesus Christ!

TEACHING MOMENTS FROM THYATIRA

1. What can be learned from the church in Thyatira?

2. Is your church being corrupted by a "watered down" version of the Gospel and the people led astray by the spirit of Jezebel in your church?

3. The glory of the Lord God is seen in the Son. How is the church responding to the true Gospel? Is the path your church is following the Gospel or the world?

Let Us Pray:

Heavenly Father, You alone are glorious and powerful above all. Lord, leads us and guide us into all righteousness for Your name's sake and according to Your glory and honor. For You are our Savior and God. Leads us down the paths of Your Will that we may continue in Your Love. In Jesus' Name, Amen

CHAPTER 5

SARDIS: THE DEAD CHURCH

These things says He who has the seven Spirits of God and the seven stars: "I know your works, that you have a name that you are alive, but you are dead. Be watchful, and strengthen the things which remain, that are ready to die, for I have not found your works perfect before God."
(Revelation 3:1-2)

Among the cities found among the seven churches of Revelation, this church has no life in its members. Do we understand what that means for the Body of Christ? It is devastating to the testimony of Christ Himself to be associated with a church that is dead. Jesus tells this church in Sardis that they have a name of being alive, but they are dead. What does that mean? This could be that the church in Sardis is one that, despite its bustling activities, they have no Spirit and therefore it is dead. This could very well be that church which fills up with warm bodies and looks vibrant and alive whereas their hearts are weak if not dead. Appearances are everything to this church.

In today's context, these churches could be growing by leaps and bounds yet they only look to facilities and outward appearances for their rewards. I continually tell the congregation, at the church I pastor, that it is not about the church business but it is about God's vision and mission. How can a church be considered alive in Christ but still be dead? The question that needs to be asked is whether or for what reason are they there. Does your congregation know the vision and mission of the church and does it line up with that of the Holy Spirit? The saddest sight is that of a church that has closed its doors and the church is in disrepair and crumbling down. One can only imagine what that church used to be like. Was the church active and vibrant or was it filled with young children and families? Generations of Spirit-filled Christians who loved to serve the Lord with all their heart, mind, soul, and strength. But, because the Spirit of God had left the people, the building becomes an abandoned shell of a structure. Is this characteristic of our life as Christians?

Jesus tells the angel of the church in Sardis to strengthen those things that remain. The message here must be never to give up, regardless, because the Holy Spirit will never give up on you. The inference here is that at one time the church was an exciting and possibly growing congregation striving for the things of God. It seems that the church has lost its spiritual perspective and needs to reset its foundation. When a church is considered dead, I see that as one which no longer considers the Spirit of God relevant. It is a church, today, that says the Bible is only a book of old stories and the God of the Bible was different than the God of today. Also, these churches may consider miracles only real to the Old and New Testaments and not relevant today. To the faithful and spiritually connected Christian, these should be disturbing on many levels. If these are characteristics of your church, then why are you there?

Remember therefore how you have received and heard; hold fast and repent. Therefore if you will not watch, I will come upon you as a thief, and you will not know what hour I will come upon you. (Revelation 3:3)

The church in Sardis seems to reflect a lethargic sense of spirituality. The church must have received messages from many prominent prophets, pastors and evangelists. Jesus is telling them to remember how they received and heard those messages. Then, He tells them that they must hold fast and repent. The messages must have been true or He would not have told them to hold fast to it. When someone holds fast, they are holding it with everything. They are not just holding it with a hand or even both hands. The whole body and soul is involved. We find strength in the power and guidance of the Holy Spirit. Whether spiritual, physical, or emotional, Jesus shows that has empowered His people for service. As we look for His immediate return, there seems to be much we all need to learn concerning the enduring steadfastness of our resolve.

SARDIS: SLEEPING AS GOOD AS DEAD

Watch and pray, lest you enter into temptation.
The spirit indeed is willing, but the flesh is weak.
(Matthew 26:41)

The deadness found in churches was even evident within the inner circle of disciples. Take note of the final moments Jesus spent in prayer. It was a night that was shrouded in darkness and deception. The disciples succumb in their weakness because of the lack of understanding concerning the true nature of the Christ and His mission. Jesus shared with His chosen twelve disciples during His last supper with them some last words and a last prediction about His death. This was the Passover meal. He washed the disciples' feet (John 13). Then, Jesus was betrayed by Judas Iscariot to the chief priests for thirty pieces of silver. Despite all that occurred over the previous week, Jesus stayed the course as God the Father had designed.

Then Jesus came with them to a place called
Gethsemane, and said to the disciples, "Sit
here while I go and pray over there." And He
took with Him Peter and the two sons of Zebe-
dee, and He began to be sorrowful and deeply
distressed. Then He said to them, "My soul is ex-

ceedingly sorrowful, even to death. Stay here and
watch with Me." (Matthew 26:36-38)

The final moments in the Garden of Gethsemane gave to the most glorious event in Christian history. He told His disciples to stay in that place and watch while He prays. They had a simple task. We have a simple task! He has asked us to watch and pray until He returns. When they were supposedly watching while He was praying, they fell asleep. Is that not characteristic of the dead church? Jesus tells us that He is going back to the Father on our behalf. We are to watch and wait for His return. Jesus told the disciples that His soul was sorrowful even unto death. This is the concern. He is not really distressed for Himself because He knows the plan for Him. It is the distress concerning the disciples. They cannot even stay awake while He walks over a stone's throw from them and prays for them. I see that the real concern with Jesus was not for His life but for *their* lives and *their* souls. It has always been about our souls. All they were told to do was to stay, watch and wait. We stand on the edge of eternity. Jesus Christ the Son of God tells us to watch and wait for Him while He goes to the Father and prepares a place.

> *Then He came to the disciples and found them*
> *sleeping, and said to Peter, "What! Could you*
> *not watch with Me one hour? Watch and pray,*
> *lest you enter into temptation. The spirit indeed*
> *is willing, but the flesh is weak."*
> (Matthew 26:40-41)

When you are in church, how often do you fall asleep during a sermon? Why do you fall asleep? Is it boring or are you just tired from the night before? The pastor sees the faces of those who sit before them. I have concluded that the people of God become content and comfortable in God's house. If this is true, I do not know.

It makes me feel better when I am preaching or teaching. Jesus told His disciples to watch and pray. This was a simple command. He also told them why. He said for them to watch and pray so that they would not enter temptation. We should be on our guard because the adversary is prowling around looking for those who are asleep and have their spiritual guard down. We, as the people of God, are chosen to be His children by His marvelous grace and mercy. Therefore, as people of God through the Blood of Jesus Christ by the power of the Holy Spirit, we should be watchful, alert and prepared for the attacks. We have been given the Holy Spirit as the means to serve Him in spirit and truth. Why do we fall asleep? A sign of a dead church is one whose congregation spiritually sleeps. If they physically sleep, then they are not receiving the message brought to them.

Again, a second time, He went away and prayed,
saying, "O My Father, if this cup cannot pass
away from Me unless I drink it, Your will be
done." And He came and found them asleep
again, for their eyes were heavy.
(Matthew 26:42-43)

Jesus told them a second time to not sleep but watch and pray. I believe that even the disciples did not understand the depths of what was happening that night. The entirety of the mission of God what unfolding before their eyes and they were oblivious to it. Is this the case for the church today? Are we fully comprehending that Jesus will come back any time and we need to be prepared? With all that is happening in the lives of those who declare themselves as Christians, there are enormous distractions that cause the church to begin to sleep and be prepared for His return. Just as crucial, are the preparation for the attacks of the adversary. When Jesus went away a second time to pray, He told them the same thing. He wanted them to be alert because they did not know when He would return and they would mindful of the enemy in the approach.

The cup that Jesus was referring to is the cup of death and sacrifice. But, it was His will and the will of the Father for the mission to be completed. Even though we may sleep, Jesus loves us and calls us to awake and be alert. If the church is not alert, then they will easily be taken down by the enemy. The real tragedy is that when we are asleep in the church is the time we will miss the return of the Lord. These are the ones who will look around and say to the Him, "Lord, Lord! Did I not heal people in Your name? Did I not cast out demons in Your name? Did I not serve the poor, clothe the naked, and visit the prison in Your name?" Then, He will turn to you and say, "Depart from Me for I never knew you!" The most devastating words that a Christian will ever hear. If we are asleep, we are not serving and loving the Lord all our heart, mind, soul and strength and loving one another as Christ loves us. Then, above all things, our testimony is false. Do you really want Jesus to find you asleep in the spirit?

SARDIS: REMNANT OF THE LIVING AND FAITHFUL

You have a few names even in Sardis who have not defiled their garments; and they shall walk with Me in white, for they are worthy. He who overcomes shall be clothed in white garments, and I will not blot out his name from the Book of Life; but I will confess his name before My Father and before His angels. (Revelation 3:4-5)

To be considered worthy before God the Father we should not defile our garments. What does this mean? If you walk in disobedience before the Lord, we have defiled the garments he has given us. When we give our hearts to the Lord, we are covered in the garment of His blood that is pure before God the Father. It was the ultimate sacrifice to God once and for all. When the church is asleep and dead in the spirit, they have taken the garment of the salvation, thrown it into the mud and walked on it. When the garment of sacrifice is taken off it makes you vulnerable to attack and therefore you are weakened. Jesus is stating that there are those within the church in Sardis who are faithful and true. These have not defiled the garments given to them through the sacrifice of Jesus. He says that these individuals' names will not be blotted out of the Book of Life. How many reading this right now want their names to be blotted out or removed from the Book of Life? I dare say that none of us!

The true Believer who walks in obedience to the Father and wears the garments that are white, will see the Kingdom of God in all its glory. Jesus said in this passage that He will confess you before the Father! If we are awake and profess Him before men. What motivates people to actively pursue God? Fear of death? Maybe it is fear of life? The pursuit of God should be the celebration of life and then we can celebrate and rejoice in death. Do you want to be considered worthy to enter into the presence of God and worthy for Jesus to confess you before the Father?

Blessed are the pure in heart,
For they shall see God. (Matthew 5:8)

If there is a beauty in the service to God the Father, it is found in the pure heart. Jesus told the disciples that the one who has a pure heart before God is Blessed. Also, that person will see God. We can stand before a Holy God and righteous God because we have a pure heart! This is how we become worthy before God. By this time in the Beatitudes, it is a crucial time in the life of the Believer that dictates the beauty of the relationship of the Believer to Jesus. The relationship is more intimate than any other time in their life. The pure heart allows the individual to see God clearly and distinctly. The person in turn will also be able to see the world through the eyes of the Holy Spirit and can serve from the heart of God. The Believer with a pure heart is therefore found worthy and the Lord Jesus will profess that person before the Father.

Jesus, when He is speaking to the Apostle John concerning the revelation to the churches, speaks to those in the church of Sardis who are sleeping to awake. The church today needs to awake and see that the righteousness of God and the Kingdom of God are the same today as they were two thousand years or even ten thousand years ago. God has not changed in His purpose. It is humanity who boxed up God and put Him away only to pull Him out when they need Him and in the way that they want to use Him. The Sardinian congregation's greatest problem was found with the spirit of apathy. Because of the brutal tortures and persecutions of Christians under the Emperor Domitian and his regime, it seems that the church in Sardis mostly just gave up. I know that God never gives up on us even when we walk away from Him. When Jesus is speaking of this church, there is still hope even in the such brutality and chaos. He speaks to those who in the end will overcome the persecutions. They will be made whole and pure white will the garments be before God and their names will not be blotted from the Book of Life. The one who follows Him with a pure heart, Matthew 5:8, will see God. If you are able to see God, then it seems to follow that you will legitimately walk in His presence and in His glory forever.

The church in Sardis was a dead church, spiritually, but this does not mean that they are a lost cause. The city of Sardis was one of immense power and wealth. Because of their general location, the city was subject to great earthquakes. The earthquakes each time devastated city along with a massive number of inhabitants. Sardis would fall, almost out of existence, then they would pick up the pieces and begin again. This seemed to be the mentality engrained in the psyche of the people of Sardis and this fear was part of the lack of spiritual health in the church, fear and hope-lessness. Jesus wanted these people to overcome the adversity to be conquerors. He gave them hope and a reason to come back to life. We as Christians in the modern era need to truly consider Jesus' words concerning this church. There is no record concerning the impact the letter made on the people of the church or the city. How does this church in Sardis and Jesus' concern effect you and your church today?

HOW FAR ARE WE OFF TARGET?

Rejoice and be exceedingly glad, for great is your reward in heaven, for so they persecuted the prophets who were before you. (Matthew 5:12)

The church which identifies with the church in Sardis needs to learn from the people of that congregation. Jesus gave them hope where there was none. So, we also have hope as long as we can hold fast to the testimony of life. Otherwise, the church will spiritually die a truly needless death. There is no need for a church to close the doors and crumble to the ground. We perish because of the lack of faith. He told the people in that church the same message He gives to us today. The message to be conquerors and overcomers by the Word of God through the power of the Holy Spirit.

Jesus told His disciples on the Sermon on the Mount to rejoice and be glad. I am sure the newly chosen disciples probably looked at Him with blank expressions that bordered amusing if it wasn't so serious. He took them on a journey so incredible that I am sure when they looked back in later years all they could do was shake their heads and smile.

This is My commandment, that you love one another as I have loved you. Greater love has no one than this, than to lay down one's life for his friends. (John 15:12-13)

Everything that Jesus had taught them from the time they met Him, finally made sense. On that glorious day of Pentecost, the Spirit of God was poured out onto those who were in that upper room and the world would not be the same. All of Jesus' teachings and His leadership, difficult as they were at times, made perfect sense at that moment. Jesus said that His commandment for the disciples was for them to love one another as He has loved them. The next statement took the commandment a step farther when He said that this may even mean to the death. His final teaching for the disciples was that He would lay down His life for them as an example. Therefore, they should love one another and be willing to do the same. The church in Sardis may have been dead in the eyes of the Lord, but He also saw that it was not beyond resurrection. The same is true for the church today. Does your church seem popular in the community, yet it is hollow inside? Spiritual death is real. It not only occurs in the person, but it also happens and is very prevalent in the church. Remember that it is because of Jesus Christ and the sacrifice He made for all, that we are be called children of God. The church is the Bride of Christ. We cannot give up and give in to hopelessness and despair. Christ did not give up on us. Eeven in two thousand years, He sees your need and the need of your church. He wants the church, the Body of Christ, to be alive and thriving. Seek the Lord while He can be found and submit to the power and authority of the Holy Spirit and the church will be delivered from death to life.

TEACHING MOMENTS FROM SARDIS

1. The church is the Body of Christ and must be alive in Christ to survive. How alive in Christ is your church?

2. Is your church an organized social club? Is your church trying to live for the glory of Christ or the glory of themselves?

3. Is your church sleeping, in a coma, or is it dying? Let the Lord revive it today!

Let Us Pray:

Heavenly Father, You are Lord of the living and the dead, You put life back into Lazarus as a testimony to Your power and glory. Father, bring life back into your people just as you did in Your Son Jesus Christ our Lord and Savior. Lord, strengthen the Body of Christ to be the Bride You have called us out to be. Lord, to You be the Glory, Honor and Praise forever. In Jesus' name, Amen

CHAPTER 6

PHILADELPHIA: THE LOYAL AND FAITHFUL

*These things says He who is holy, He who is true,
"He who has the key of David, He who opens
and no one shuts, and shuts and no one opens":
"I know your works. See, I have set before you an
open door, and no one can shut it; for you have a
little strength, have kept My word, and have not
denied My name.* (Revelation 3:7-8)

The church in the city of Philadelphia is understood as the most faithful of all the churches of the seven. Why? Because they were faithful. This does not mean they were perfect. As we see today, particularly in spiritual circles, there are no perfect churches. There seems to be a note of humility, even though Jesus does not say it. It is implied in the manner and way of His description of the church. The description of Himself that He provides John says much to the character of the church. This is because Jesus says that He is holy and true. If you are looking in the face of a holy and true God, then the person or persons should be faithful themselves. He also says that He has the key of David. The key, I believe, is to God's own heart.

The key of David, he was a man after God's own heart, is the key to God's heart. Are we as a church wanting and desiring the door to God's heart be opened to us. The church in Philadelphia was given the key to God's own heart, as David. Jesus said that He had the power to open and to close it. He has the authority over all things. He goes on to say that He knows their works and that He

has set before them an open door that no one can shut. Nobody but
God alone has control over the things of God except God Himself.
When a church is shown favor by God, there are great spiritual
works that are in progress. Even in the frail state of the human heart
and mind because of the sinful nature that taints the perfect image
of God created in us, He gives strength in our weaknesses. As we
take a closer look at the church in Philadelphia, we need to take
note of the fact that it is their humility, faithfulness, and meekness
that set them apart. They seem to display an understanding of the
Beatitudes unmatched by the other churches.

PHILADELPHIA: THE HUMBLE PEOPLE

Blessed are the poor in spirit,
For theirs is the kingdom of heaven.
(Matthew 5:3)

The humble spirit is one that recognizes the truth in the fact
that we are nothing in the hands of a holy God. But, Jesus said
that in our weakness He is strong. We find our strength in Him
through the power of the Holy Spirit in our lives. The Believer
who truly puts aside their own spirit and will for that of the Lord
will receive the Kingdom of God as an inheritance. The beauty
of that inheritance is that they live in the glory of the living God.
Your life was never promised to be perfect and without problems.
We see in the humility found within the church in Philadelphia
a unique connection to those who are willing to sacrifice in times
of persecution and chaos. Like the church in Smyrna, the church
in Philadelphia finds itself overwhelmed with the culture and all
its trappings. The Greek culture was dominating in the city and
therefore the influences of the pantheons of gods and goddesses is
what controlled the climate of the day. Because of these culturally
diverse philosophies and religious stature it was considered as "little
Athens" because of the many temples that adorn the city. Despite

the religious strengths of the city, the Christian church was strong spiritually.

Humility is the power found within any congregation. The world and all its trappings see humility and humble acts as weaknesses, but the Lord sees power and strength. When the Lord tells John that this church has little strength, it is referring to their poverty monetarily. This area, as most in the region, is prone to constant earthquakes. It was difficult for the citizens to maintain any form of stability. The church itself was poor monetarily, but they were strong in their faith in the Lord. Humility is one of the hallmarks of the church in Philadelphia and this was what set them apart and made them unique. For this reason, a bishop was established in the church to oversee the maintaining of the church. The beauty of the church was its unwavering faithful to the Lord Jesus Christ and His mission.

PHILADELPHIA: REWARDED AS FAITHFUL

Indeed I will make those of the synagogue of Satan, who say they are Jews and are not, but lie—indeed I will make them come and worship before your feet, and to know that I have loved you. Because you have kept My command to persevere, I also will keep you from the hour of trial which shall come upon the whole world, to test those who dwell on the earth.
(Revelation 3:9-10)

The synagogue of Satan, as the Jews are being referred, is the one that caused so much turmoil within the churches for years. The churches' responses, throughout the region, were all different because of the mentality of the people and their influences. The Lord makes a point in distinguishing this church and setting them apart from the others as examples to them. The church in Philadelphia was truly faithful in all respects so their enemies would be made to come and worship at their feet. This statement is a testimony to their commitment despite any physical and spiritual attacks. When some of the other churches would crumble and succumb to the temptations and influences of the world around them, this church stood their ground and remained faithful. God often told His people that if they would worship Him and Him alone then He would make their enemies their footstool.

The declaration of the Lord to this church that their enemies was not the only portion. The enemies that Jesus is speaking about are those Jews who have dedicated their lives to upholding Judaism as the standard for all Christians. These Jews He refers to as the "synagogue of Satan." This is extremely telling considering that He is speaking about who are the chosen people of God. This is a powerful statement and should be considered when questioning Christ's love for us. The church in Philadelphia, being far from perfect, was the closest example of a holy congregation. Many people believe that God has shown favorites with the Jewish nation, but one would consider that God has a much longer history with this nation. They are chosen, but all the nations now included. Does this mean that loves them more? No, by no means! Consider the parable of the vineyard and the workers that Jesus told.

GROUP #1

For the kingdom of heaven is like a landowner who went out early in the morning to hire laborers for his vineyard. Now when he had agreed with the laborers for a denarius a day, he sent them into his vineyard. (Matthew 20:1-2)

The first group to be chosen as God's most precious creation was Adam and Eve. Being the first people created, they were originally declared as good. This, of course, changed with the fall as sin entered in the once perfect creation. Those who were hired in the morning, first thing, agreed to the terms of their hire and was faithful in their job. They served the vineyard owner and served well until the conditions and results did not seem to match with the terms as they perceived them. The terms were simple. They agreed to work the day in the vineyard and the wages were to be a denarius, a normal full days wage. Adam and Eve, following their creation, were called to care for the garden. They were only given one restriction. Otherwise, they had full consideration over the care of the garden and its inhabitants. They failed to comply to the one restriction and was then cast from the garden. It was their disobedience that set the rejection of God and His love. From this rejection, sin was introduced into an otherwise perfect and good creation.

GROUP #2

---

*And he went out about the third hour and saw
others standing idle in the marketplace, 4 and
said to them, 'You also go into the vineyard, and
whatever is right I will give you.' So they went.*
(Matthew 20:3-4)

The second initial group of workers hired in the third hour are like the Jewish people who are those called from Abraham and Sarah. These were the first chosen by God to be His people and He will be their God. They were chosen as the first generational line selected to be God's people, following the flood. They were called to be the priesthood to all the nations. As was seen with those who were selected in the third hour, it was clear that God had made an agreement with these as well. The agreement or covenant God made with the people was basically the same in that He would be their God and they would be His people. Because of their rebellion of the rules, terms and conditions set place, at the end of the day, they would receive the same wage for their service. As this group began to grow and multiply on the earth, it was overwhelming for those of the worldly kingdoms who tried confine and control them. Sin began to penetrate even the most sacred of people. These people were called out from among the nations to serve God and no other. Because of their sin, God allowed them to be swallowed into a dominating culture that made slaves. Following fourteen generations, God decided to deliver them from their bonds and renew the task at hand. This leads to group three or the group with a changed heart toward God. He answered their cries and called them out.

GROUP #3

Again he went out about the sixth and the ninth hour, and did likewise. And about the eleventh hour he went out and found others standing idle, and said to them, 'Why have you been standing here idle all day?' They said to him, 'Because no one hired us.' He said to them, 'You also go into the vineyard, and whatever is right you will receive. (Matthew 20:5-7)

Various times in God's salvation history, He called His people out of the darkness and gave them opportunity be to reconciled back to Him. With this third group, God set the rules and regulations in place on stone tablets. The eternal result is still the same and the players are the same, but God has given them a new standard to make it easier to recognize the sin. The eternal goal for God never has changed. He works to address the needs of His chosen people. In the parable of the vineyard, Jesus is relaying a story that speaks to the human condition. Humans have a difficult time with authority and how that interacts in life. From the very beginning, God wanted His creation to worship, love and serve Him. In these remaining three groups, Jesus gives the implication that all these are paid the same, regardless of time spent. The result is the same for the last group as it was for the first. As was the result, the first groups did not think it to be fair those who were called the latest to be given the same wage as those who were hired first. The Jews were first as the chosen people of God.

The goal for God to the world is eternal life. God's goal for humanity is reconciliation with Him and eternal salvation. Those who entered at the eleventh hour are the ones considered Christians. This means that God wants all humanity to truly reconciled back to Him.

---

*So the last will be first, and the first last. For
many are called, but few chosen."*
(Matthew 20:16)

We are the last to enter the eternal equation with the introduction of the Son of God. God love the entire world so much that He sent His only Son so that no one would die but that they would have eternal life (John 3:16). The indicators given by Jesus both in the Matthew and the Revelation passages give the Believer the hope that regardless to where they fall on the timeline of humanity, it is God who is in control. Because, apart from His mercy and grace, we are bound in sin and death.

WHAT DOES THIS PARABLE HAVE TO DO WITH CHRISTIANS TODAY?

The glorious of salvation can be seen in the end with the parable of the vineyard and the workers. The Jewish people consider themselves secured in the front row of eternity. They believe that since they are considered God's "chosen people" from the beginning, then they are entitled to their promised place in eternity. This is true. But, we need to consider that Jesus said that few will enter through the narrow gate that leads to salvation. The various groups of individuals in this parable all came to work toward a single goal.

They each agreed on a wage. Whether they came began work for the Kingdom from the beginning or came to the vineyard in the eleventh hour of the day, the end wage was the same, eternal life. Jesus had this conversation with the disciples concerning who will be the greatest in the kingdom. Just because you were with Him from the beginning does not mean that you are entitled to a seat at the right hand of privilege. Jesus also told the disciples that even He was called not to be served but to serve. Just because you gave your life to Jesus at twelve years old and die at one hundred does not put you in a better position than one who gives their life to Jesus on their deathbed. That is for God to judge.

The church in Philadelphia was faithful and true to living the gospel of Christ amid turmoil and chaos. The Jewish Christians considered themselves entitled to the grace and glory of God because of their heritage and possible connection with the Jewish Jesus. When considering the Gentile Christians in Philadelphia, they were humbled by their position in the kingdom of God. This gave them a much greater consideration. The first shall be last and the last shall be first. As was indicated earlier, the workers in the vineyard, regardless of the time they began, agreed on a wage. The end was the same. Eternal life is the end for the Christian, Jew or Gentile Christian, is does not matter. When we can get passed the concerns for entitlements and lineage and privileges, then we will be able to see the kingdom of God and be assured of the salvation given to us.

PHILADELPHIA: THE PILLARS OF THE KINGDOM

Behold, I am coming quickly! Hold fast what you have, that no one may take your crown. He who overcomes, I will make him a pillar in the Temple of God, and he shall go out no more. I will write on him the name of my God and the name of the city of My God, the New Jerusalem, which

> *comes down out of heaven from My God. And I*
> *will write on him My new name.*
> (Revelation 3:11-12)

Jesus wants us to be prepared in all things. He wants His people that call on Him to hold on to the testimony because the crown of life is ours. The crown is not ours instead of the Jews because of their unfaithfulness, it is ours along with our Jewish brothers and sisters who seek Jesus with all their hearts. He is telling the church today to be ready and to stand fast and strong even in difficult times. Because, the overcomers will become pillars in the Temple of God. If you want to be first in the Kingdom of God, then you must be last. Despite all the trappings and influences of the world around you, there is a steadfast strength that stands before all and that is the hope of eternal life. In these two verses, the greatest promises God gives are found. What a privilege that God gives the faithful power, authority, and knowledge in the Kingdom of God. Nowhere else in Scripture does God give this kind of promise. He makes the faithful a pillar, or person of authority. Also, He said that He would give you eternal rest and you would not go out any more. Then, above all, He will give you a new name, the name of the city of God, the New Jerusalem, and the name of God Himself. With these are given an authoritative place of authority never promised previously.

Remember, when we see Jesus coming again in the clouds with His armies and calling His people home, He has a name written on His thigh that nobody knows but Him. He told the church that those who overcome will know His name. Wow! The beginning of verse eleven gives the key, to be ready. Are we ready for the coming of the Lord Jesus Christ? He said to "Behold" or look and watch! Be mindful of everything around you, what you say and your actions. Do not let the world dictate your eternity. He said that you need to hold fast and strong for the time of His coming is approaching. The beauty found in the church of Philadelphia is in its single-mindedness and focus on the things of God, despite those who tried within to destroy their testimony. To be a pillar in the Temple of God, means that you are to be closer to God and His throne and in a place of authority than anyone, except Jesus Christ His Son. This is given as a great place of honor in the presence of God and before His throne.

HOW FAR ARE WE OFF TARGET?

Blessed are the pure in heart,
for they shall see God.
Blessed are the peacemakers, for they shall be
called the sons of God.
(Matthew 5:8-9)

Jesus, when He began His earthly ministry, laid the foundation for a blessed and holy life before God the Father. Throughout the remainder of His ministry, He demonstrated those standards. The church in Philadelphia lived per the standard set in place and lived out by Jesus. Should they receive the same wage than those of the Jewish people chosen from the beginning? I do not believe it is seniority more than it is obedience and faithfulness to the commands and statutes of God the Father through the Son and by the work of the Holy Spirit. Then, the question needs to be considered as we attempt to strive for the life God has called us, how are we living this life? If you want to know how far you are off target with God's plan, consider the spiritual mirror of your life. Do you yourself or do you see Jesus? How you see your spiritual walk with Jesus is reflected in the way you conduct your and how others perceive Jesus through you. It is never about you because it is always about Him. The people in the body of Christ are His ambassadors to the lost world. The church in Philadelphia was strong and faithful so Jesus the depths of their love for Him. If we need to ask the question of how far are we off target, then chances are that we need to reevaluate our relationship with Jesus as well as the church as being the

Body of Christ. When the city of Philadelphia was established and built by the king of Pergamos, Eucomus, for his brother Attachus III, he did so as a testimony to the love for his brother. It is truly ironic that the church established in that city three hundred years later would be also be considered by Jesus, the Son of God, as the pillar of brotherly love and a Godly example for others to follow.

TEACHING MOMENTS IN PHILADELPHIA

1. This is one church that Jesus did not expose any fault in. Looking to the church in Philadelphia, how should we model our churches today?

2. Knowing that there are no perfect churches, what do you think is a possible weakness in this church and how can this prove as an important teaching tool for your church?

3. The parable of the laborers in the vineyard is a telling parable of our commitment to the work of the gospel of Christ. Looking at each of the three groups who were hired by the land owner, how do they reflect those in your congregation?

4. How are you going to use the example of the church in Philadelphia as the example of the church that God calls good in His sight?

Let us Pray:

O Most Heavenly Father, Gracious Lord, leads us, I pray down the paths of Your righteousness for Your name's sake. Lord, through Your Holy Spirit, teach to become the faithful and loyal pillars of the kingdom that You have called us to be. For it I for Your glory and Yours alone that we serve You in spirit and in truth. In the name of the Father, the Son, and of the Holy Spirit. In Jesus' name, Amen.

CHAPTER 7

LAODICEA: THE LUKE WARM CHURCH

*So then, because you are lukewarm, and neither
cold nor hot, I will vomit you out of My mouth.*
(Revelation 3:16)

For over two millennia, the church has been battling for supremacy on the world stage. The cyclical fluctuation between good and evil has not only been expressed in the world with various religious wars and causes to bring the annihilation of one faction or the other. But, within the church lies as much deceit and conceit to find at its core where the devil himself would truly find a home. Jesus said to His disciples that they are not of this world but they are in the world. They will be hated by the world for His name sake. So, the church falls into the ever-spiraling pattern that sends them closer to the gates of hell rather than the pearly gates of heaven. To the casual observer, neither good nor evil are better or worse than the other. This means that it does not look good for those who believe their eternity is sure. If the church looks no different than the world around it, then the Spirit of God has no part in it.

As the Lord begins to open our eyes to the true church, we will learn that we, as a community of Believers, have been wondering aimlessly in the world of misinterpretation and severe misunderstanding of God's cosmic plans for humanity. There has been more wars and crimes against humanity seen within the church than ever there was outside. As Believers in Jesus Christ, we need to understand that God is not the one at fault. We are our own worst enemy. As a community of Believers, we stand at the edge of the great gulf of eternity waiting eagerly for the coming of our Lord Jesus while we are turning our backs on Him and escorting the adversary into the heart of our lives. The battle lines have been drawn and it is now time for humanity to make the ultimate choice – for real!

The seven churches of Jesus' revelation to John the Apostle paints a different portrait of the character and the condition of the church, the "Bride of Christ." The church at Laodicea was selected for discussion because it brings to the surface the worst state of the church. Ironically, these churches are among the most successful in terms of profit and numbers.

LAODICEA: EVERYBODY'S CHURCH

I know thy works, that thou art neither cold nor hot: I would thou wert cold or hot. So then because thou art lukewarm, and neither cold nor hot, I will spew you out of my mouth.
(Revelation 3:15-16)

Jesus told His people throughout history that hard times would come and they would turn away in the good times believing that they would not need God. Look at the Apostle Peter. The rock of the Apostles, as Jesus made note, but he was human. Peter walked on water to Jesus. He was a member of Jesus' inner circle of disciples. Peter was also the first to stand and fight for Jesus when He was seized by the temple guard prior to His crucifixion. But, he also was the first among the inner circle to deny he ever knew Jesus. Yes, he was human. Yes, Jesus came back following His resurrection and forgave him. Following the outpouring of the Holy Spirit, Peter was the first to stand and speak to the multitudes concerning Jesus as the Son of God. So, let us take a long hard look at the position of the "Body of Christ" as we know it and as Jesus sees it beginning with the church in Laodicea, the last of the seven churches of Revelation. Sadly, this church does reveal to us the condition and path of the present day mainline churches. May we take heed and turn back to God before it is too late.

The city of Laodicea was founded in 250B.C. by King Antiochus II of which he named for his wife Laodice. He populated the city with imported Syrians and Jews for a purpose and strategy for the region. The region, through the financial and banking strategies of the Jews and farming and cultural techniques of the Syrians, was the wealthiest city in Asia Minor. Black wool and fine purple linens were their specialties. They excelled and were known throughout the world. Their location, in short proximity to much larger major "hub" cities such as Ephesus, contributed to their religious and political strong ties as well. Even though the church in Laodicea was very successful in terms of numbers, it's stands on the issues that mattered and the fundamentals of Christianity, set them in the category being classified as a "moderate" in modern terms.

In today's world, the tolerant and touchy, feely church may see this as a good thing or even best option out there. This is truly the worst possible choice. A moderate is a fence rider. This is a church that sees no distinction between good and evil or right or wrong. They are "middle-of-the-road" Believers. Grey areas dominate every aspect of their belief system, whether religious, spiritual, or political. There are no distinctions. Outwardly, they may follow toward one extreme or the other. But, they are aiming for the bottom line in terms of popularity and numbers. The "mainline" churches and most "mega" churches, at their very core, sadly fall into this classification. Many misinterpret fast growth with blessing, when in fact it is the work of great marketing strategies and motivational speakers. These churches are very busy in their outreaches and extreme causes for the good of the community. They develop "programs" aimed at reaching target groups, rather than "ministries" aimed at leading souls into a relationship with Jesus Christ. This classification is not solely dedicated to just those large churches, but there are smaller churches that fall under that deception as well. They look to the larger churches for guidance and mentorship, so in turn they incorporate the ideas and programs into their own plan for church growth. It is not the quality of life and growth found in the relationship with Jesus Christ that is important, but the quantity of bodies to fill the pews.

Understanding the moderate point of view is not very difficult once you stand outside the box and view it objectively. Comments I have heard from within and outside those congregations are basically that they are cold and very regimented in their methods. Legalism and formalism is found at their core values. All of this is taught and enforced in the name of Jesus Christ. Around 90% of the church's membership are going through the motions and don't attend Sunday School or Bible study. Many scholars and commentators consider the church at Laodicea an example of the present-day church. I believe that it is much more. It is the worst form of apostasy and hypocrisy seen to date and all in the name of Jesus Christ. What is at the core of their beliefs is the idea of tolerance. Many churches twist the phrase "Hate the sin, but love the sinner" into crusades for acceptance of most abominations listed in Scripture. So, as can be noted, being a moderate before God is not good because that church is easily swayed with every movement of the wind. Remember our Lord's statement to the church in Laodicea:

". . . because thou art lukewarm, and neither
cold nor hot, I will spew you out of my mouth."
(Revelation 3:16)

Consider the thought, when you drink something like milk, for example, you expect it to be cold and fresh. What if you picked up that glass of milk and it was room temperature and spoiled with a sour smell and taste. Your reaction is to violently spit it out, if not vomit as well, considering your constitution. This is the church as a rancid, spoiled smell and taste to the senses of God. It repels the workings of the Holy Spirit from ever manifesting within that body of Believers. When a person is proud to be considered as a moderate in their beliefs, they tend to become whatever the world wants them to become. At least someone who is cold toward their belief in Christ is firm in their decision and not just following the most popular theme of the day.

When Christians look at their lives, they do not seem to look deep enough to truly see what drives their most basis beliefs. Jesus, in Matthew 25:31 – 46, gives the reader a vivid depiction and extremely disturbing account of the separation between those who are hot, those who are surrendered to the Lord, and everyone else.

When the Son of Man shall come in His glory,
and all the holy angels with Him, then shall
He sit upon the throne of His glory: And before
Him shall be gathered all nations: and He shall
separate them one from another, as a shepherd
divideth His sheep from the goats: And He shall
set the sheep on His right hand, and the goats on
His left. (Matthew 25:31-33)

He is separating the sheep from the goats or those who truly serve Him in Spirit and truth, and those who are merely going through the motions. The sheep and the goats are both considered Believers in Christ. One group, the sheep, were humble, merciful, and Christ-like. The other group, the goats, were going through the motions and, by all accounts truly good people, but ultimately sought their own glory and shared none with Christ. As you can see, this is the church at large today. Divided, segregated, and by all intent and purposes, being destroyed from within by its own worldly tolerances and stances. When the church is judged, it is not judged wholly, but each individual soul is held in account. This is not only true for your life but for all those souls that you have influenced. Scary, huh?

Remember that next time you serve halfheartedly or feel it to be an obligation or "job" to serve and care for others. Jesus, with every step He took as He struggled up the road to the cross, did so out of pure unconditional love for you and me. Consider the fact that there is no possible way that you could repay Him for His sacrifice. All He wants from you is love and praise, and for those who do to serve and love Him with all their heart, mind, soul and strength. The apostle Paul said it well in his letter to the Philippian church:

Let nothing be done through strife or vainglory; but in lowliness of mind let each esteem other better than themselves. Look not every man on his own things, but every man also on the things of others. Let this mind be in you, which was also in Christ Jesus: Who, being in the form of God, thought it not robbery to be equal with God: But made Himself of no reputation, and took upon Him the form of a servant, and was made in the likeness of men: And being found in fashion as a man, He humbled Himself, and became obedient unto death, even the death of the cross. (Philippians 2:3-8)

Found within these five glorious verses in the letter to the Philippian church is the same characteristics that Jesus taught and demonstrated to His disciples from the beginning of His ministry in Matthew chapter five. The Beatitudes are levels in the continuing process of growth from the infancy of our conversion and justification through an entire life toward sanctification until the Christian can be with the Lord forever in glorification. But, unfortunately, most Christian Believers fall into the "lukewarm" or "moderate" category. If this is true, then the bride is ill prepared for the coming of the Bridegroom and she needs to turn her eyes away from the workings and glories of the world and focus once again on Jesus Christ through the power of the Holy Spirit for guidance.

LAODICEA: SPIRITUALLY POOR CHURCH

Because thou sayest, I am rich, and increased
with goods, and have no need of nothing;
and knowest not that thou art wretched, and
miserable, and poor, and blind, and naked:
(Revelation 3:17)

Jesus did not mix His words when revealing this to John. The Laodicean church was so caught up in the game of self-glorification and self-righteousness that they did not even see that they were blazing a direct path for the gates of hell. They were narrow-mindedly moralistic in many aspects. Their culture was inbred with the surrounding cities and cultures to the point that there was no real separation of right or wrong and moral or immoral. The lines that divided them were not just blurred but erased in their belief system. There was no real distinction between the trappings of the world and the freedom of their faith. This is the travesty of the church today. The church is operating under the disillusionment and deception of the higher the tally the greater your position in heaven. If there is no plan for spiritual growth for the church and members, then they might as well become a community action group. Without a spiritual plan, the Body of Christ will wither and die to God.

Today's church, which is classified as "Laodicean," shows itself to the world through great works, but their fruit is withered and spoiled. They are so self-absorbed and self- glorified that the works of the adversary are disguised in great programs that address every physical, emotional, and mental issues in the world today. But, they are blind and deaf to the core of the problem and that is the true spiritual identity of the Body of Christ as it is intimately formed into the Bride adorned for the Bridegroom.

Laodicea was truly a wealthy city. It was set up that way by Antiochus II. The church in Laodicea was apparently no different.

As it is today, the church was a cross section of the culture and ideologies present at the time. So, look at the modern "Christian" church and how far it has wondered off the path. Modern day tolerance and acceptance of everything opposed to the teachings of Scripture by leaders in the church and government has driven the church further and further away from God's presence and into the arms of the one who wants nothing more than to destroy us. The modern church is so caught up in what they are doing that they are forgetting the one for whom they should be serving. Jesus is revealing the heart of the problem with the church at Laodicea. Because of their indifference to the worldly activity within and outside the church, the halfhearted approach toward programs ultimately strives to glorify themselves. This church is rooted in spiritual pride and self-righteousness which is seen in their spiritual blindness, formalism, and legalism that reflects a true deep set spiritual poverty. They were spiritually impoverished, but they were truly convinced deep down in their heart that they were leaders of the pack in Christian leadership, service, and love. These modern churches fall into the same trap and therefore follow the way of the church of Laodicea.

The world sees and believes that these churches have it all figured out. But, the reality of the spiritual condition of these churches is that they are critical. They are whole bodies of Believers who are caught within a spiritual coma. These churches do not recognize the saving hand of Christ trying to reach in and pull them out to put them back on the true path to righteousness. Their lack of "Spiritual" enthusiasm and their conformity to worldly knowledge and understandings place this church and those who follow their teachings at the bottom of the heap and, in God's eyes, are unfit for the Kingdom of God. But, Jesus gives even this church a way out and a directive to be put back on the right path to righteousness.

LAODICEA: A CALL TO HUMILITY AND REPENTANCE

---

*I counsel thee to buy of me gold tried in the fire,
that thou mayest be rich; and white raiment,
that thou mayest be clothed, and that the shame
of thy nakedness do not appear; and anoint thine
eyes with eye salve, that thou mayest see. As many
as I love, I rebuke and chasten: be zealous therefore, and repent.* (Revelation 3:18-19)

The Lord knows where the heart of the problem is in the church at Laodicea, just as He knows the same for the church today. This is a call back into a relationship with Him and Him alone. He said that He counsels them. The Lord in these few words speaks volumes to the church and their condition. The condition of the Laodicean church, as well as the churches today, are caught up in the deadly addiction of world popularity and pride. He is telling them and us that it is our choice. Jesus shows the church its deficits and sins and the church needs to accept the rebuke and repent. When He said, *"buy of me gold tried in the fire,"* He is telling the church to receive the treasures of heaven that are purified by the fire of heaven. The gold mentioned is the eternal salvation of your souls. He is not referring to lip service and outwardly appearances to appease the worldly ears. It is the fire of the Holy Spirit in the soul that purifies an otherwise tainted, putrid and sinful soul.

They can be rich in spiritual things. Even more, they can be clothed in white raiment. This is a sign of purity. A sinful soul cannot be in the presence of the Most High and Holy God. Therefore, the shamefulness and sinfulness of their spiritual nakedness will not appear before God. Likewise, the eyes are the gateway to the soul and Jesus calls the church to apply the eye salve of God. As the eyes see, so the heart does. The more the church falls on their knees and prays and studies God's Word and serves Him in fasting and worship, the more the grey areas that presently plague the church diminish.

Jesus is also offering the church in Laodicea and the modern church a call to repentance for His children. In verse nineteen, Jesus speaks to them as though He would a child of His own. His statement gives reference not only to mercy but truly to justice. Also, in verse twenty, He gives an additional approach and opportunity for them and us to repent. He says, *"Behold, I stand at the door, and knock: if any man hear My voice, and open the door, I will come in to him, and will sup with him, and he with Me."* Even as He speaks to a totally self-absorbed church, He still leaves room for grace and mercy. Jesus is standing at the doors of many churches across the United States and the world waiting for the true spiritual invitation to come in to those bodies of Believers and build on the relationship sought for in the beginning, but forgotten. His call is to the church, the people of God, not to a religion, a society, or a radical group. In 2 Chronicles 7:14, the Lord said to Solomon and His people,

---

If My people, which are called by My name, shall
humble themselves, and pray, and seek My face,
and turn from their wicked ways; then will I
hear from heaven, and will forgive their sin, and
will heal their land. (2 Chronicles 7:14)

These words, spoken by God to His people, are just as true and powerful today as they were to the Israelites and Solomon in that time. God gave His congregation four basic Beatitudes to do. In return, He would give them everything. God covered the first four Beatitudes presented by Jesus on the Mount as He taught His newly chosen disciples how to be a true follower of God. The church in Laodicea, as well as the modern mainline and mainstream churches, need to wake up, take a real hard look in the mirror that Christ has set before us and climb off the fence of moderate, tolerant religion and become on fire and hot for God. When this happens, true New Testament, Holy Spirit power will be seen and felt in the congregations of God by the people and a new age of true Holy Spirit, Son of God renewal will occur and the true Bride of Christ will rise ready for her Bridegroom. Are we ready?

How far are we off target?

THE CHURCH OF LAODICEA AND JESUS' TEACHINGS

The church in the city of Laodicea in Asia Minor gives the reader of Scripture a picture of the failings of the church. This is not only viewing the church of today but a glimpse of the failings of the church within sixty years of its inception. If we look back to Jesus and when He was teaching His disciples and the multitudes, we see a simpler and direct teaching. Jesus did not consider any gray areas. There are no exceptions to the rule. In fact, He raised the bar. The laws established by God through Moses was the standard for the Jewish people. But, Jesus told His disciples "You have heard it said" or "For it is written," but He moved the standard bar while explaining the various laws when He said to them, "But I say to you."

The bar set by the standard of Jesus was established when He opened His mouth and began to share with His disciples the eight-level characteristic process by which a person can become a true follower of Christ and a child of God. The Beatitudes was set at the beginning of Jesus' ministry to not only give the disciples, and us, a beginning but also to give the Christian the ultimate end. Each one of the characteristics that one should strive achieve, raises the bar of knowledge, understanding, and wisdom from God that the Believer would need to build an intimate relationship with the Father, through the Son and in the power of the Holy Spirit. In Jesus' short three-year ministry, He taught, lived and demonstrated all eight of these characteristics. They also gave the Believer in Jesus a base and as guide to grow in their walk with Him. The disciples of Jesus, even those closest to Him, did not understand the overall significance of what He was attempting to teach to them. Are we any more perceiving to the call of God and the direction and leadership of the Holy Spirit? Christians, as anyone today would do, tend to pick and choose how they wish to follow Jesus. Many of the Beatitudes instructed by Jesus became difficult to follow and accept. So, we find ourselves in the here today. The church in Laodicea. The world that Jesus walked was in deep need of a Savior. They needed God. But, by the time the scales fell from their eyes and they realized Jesus for who He really was it was to late. Even so, Jesus forgave them to the death on the cross!

Blessed are the poor in spirit,
For theirs is the kingdom of heaven.
(Matthew 5:3)

The knowledge of the Holiness of God is not something that can be taken lightly. The Son is the Glory of the Father and this was evidenced in His teachings. The beginning of all understanding and what is built upon as the foundation of all Jesus' teachings is humility. In all Jesus said and accomplished, He was the prime example of humility in the lives of humanity. When He began His earthly ministry with the simple statement, He rocked the foundations of the world in all belief systems and cultures of the time. The Beatitudes, especially today in the world and in the church, has been eradicated from all that is holy.

THE TEACHING MOMENTS FROM LAODICEA

1. Is your church one that follows the easy path? Does it choose the path of least resistance or make the hard choices for God?

2. Are you as a church that was founded on the principals and teachings of Christ undecided on issues crucial to the direction of the church?

3. Does the strength of your church rely on just the pastor or is your strength found in the congregation as a whole and the Holy Spirit as the center of everything and all decisions?

4. Are you willing to make God spit you out of His mouth because of the bitterness of your sin and indecision or are you going to take a stand and be on fire for God through His Son in the power of the Holy Spirit?

Let us Pray;

Father, in Heaven in pray, do not let us be directed by the adversary down the paths of unrighteousness. Lord, may we never be cold and especially lukewarm in love for You. Please guide us and direct us on Your paths of righteousness for Your Name's sake. In Jesus' Name, Amen.

CHAPTER 8

THE SPIRITUAL CHURCH: A CALL BACK TO THE TRUE SPIRITUAL BEGINNINGS

Blessed is he who reads and those who hear the words of this prophecy, and keep those things which are written in it; for the time is near.
(Revelation 1:3)

The blessings of the eternal life in Christ is the concept that many people reject because it is something that cannot be accessed using the physical senses. The definition of faith stands here as a testimony to the enduring power to overcome the evil that has plagued the world. Beauty in all its forms can be found in the created order. God's beauty and testimony is present in all we see. Every breath we breathe becomes more precious to our very core. The more we wrestle with our mortality the more God in all His glory comes into view. Jesus took the opportunity to come to John and allow him to receive this final revelation not only for the seven churches, but, more precisely, for all humanity. These churches are representations of the cultural separations of the churches, past, present, and future. Many scholars take pride in establishing various determinations concerning the revelation of Jesus to John. I do not claim to have the answers by no means. I am just offering educated theory based on study and pray led by the Holy Spirit. Also, I am not saying these ideas are correct, but they are my understanding of interestingly different way of viewing the church, the conditions and state of the church. We need to know the where we have come from to see more clearly how to proceed in the Will of God.

Jesus told the seven churches that they would be blessed if they follow three basic concepts concerning these revelations. They must first read these prophecies. Second, the reader must also hear the words. Finally, they must then keep the words in their hearts and live per their words. Why? He tells us because the time is drawing near and as we know today, the time has now come. These are not only warnings but they are encouragements to those who are suffering for the sake of the gospel of Christ. As this study begins to conclude, the questions need to be addressed that brings our true salvation into clear focus. This is because the light has come into the world and we as Christians have been given an enormous responsibility to carry the light of Jesus Christ into a dark and otherwise sinful, dead world into that light. We cannot do the task set before us on our own. It is only in the power and authority of the Holy Spirit that we can be overcomers by the Blood of the Lamb.

People in churches become fearful of those things that they cannot grasp and so the book of Revelation becomes a very fearful one to tackle. We should not fear that which God has given us. When Jesus told John the Apostle to write these things down, it was for the intent of His people to read, hear, and live by these prophecies. Every word in the Scriptures have survived for God's glory and the edification of the church and the spread of the gospel of Christ.

All Scripture is given by inspiration of God, and is profitable for doctrine, for reproof, for correction, for instruction in righteousness, that the man of God may be complete, thoroughly equipped for every good work. (2 Timothy 3:16)

The Scriptures that are given by God to His people have survived for several millennia and if anything grow in power and authority. The Scriptures are profitable for the people of God to grow into that reconciled relationship with Him that was lost long ago. It is profitable for doctrine, reproof, correction, instruction and the equipping of those for the service of God. The implication here is that Jesus says He has given us all we need to be equipped for every good work. He not only says that we will be equipped, but he says that we will be *thoroughly* equipped. This means that we have no excuse. Ignorance is not bliss when it comes to the Scripture. All these Scriptures are given so that the man of God will be complete and whole in Christ. We are made whole and complete in Christ through the teaching and guidance of the Holy Spirit by the reading, hearing, and living the word of God. Because we keep His commandments and live His statutes, then we will be considered men and women of God. As we have learned throughout this study of the seven churches of Revelation, many things have come to light concerning the condition of the church, the Bride of Christ. Knowing these teachings, we then need to them and teach others to do the same as examples.

THE SPIRITUAL CHURCH: BECOMING READERS OF THE WORD

This Book of the Law shall not depart from your mouth, but you shall meditate in it day and night, that you may observe to do according to all that is written in it. For then you will make your way prosperous, and then you will have good success. (Joshua 1:8)

The Book of the Law was of the greatest importance to the Israelites and Joshua as their newly Godly appointed leader. The law, as we as Believers in God understand it, should be just as important as is was to the Israelites. Jesus said that He did not come to abolish the law but to fulfill the law. It is God will and purpose that the word of God be followed. The people of God, Jew or Gentile, need to realize that the more we study the Scriptures inspired by God, the closer to God we grow. Many believe that the Old Testament is irrelevant to the people of God today. This is not true! Just as in the beginning was the Word, He was with God, and He was God. The same is true today. The whole Word of God is truly relevant even today. The Lord is saying to Joshua and the people of Israel that they not only should read the word but they should meditate on the word. If they would have done this through the history of God's people, they would have recognized Jesus as the Son of God. But that was the plan from the beginning. The importance of the word of God play's a crucial, if not central, role in the sanctification of the Believer to the whole relationship in Jesus Christ as the Son of God.

The writer of the Proverbs was a man of great wisdom and it was attributed to Solomon as the who was responsible for this great compilation. Solomon says that

---

"Every word of God is pure; He is a shield to
those who put their trust in Him."
(Proverbs 30:5)

The beauty of the thoughts of Solomon here is that he is truly looking at the basic purpose of God's intent for His word and how the reader should receive it. Every word of God is pure because there is no deceit found in Him. We can trust what we read in the word of God. When the word became flesh and dwelt among the creation, it was the turning point of reconciliation of the creation to the Creator. Because of this, we are to seek our refuge in the word and it is a source of strength for those of us who are weak.

"The entrance of Your words gives light; It gives
understanding to the simple." (Psalm 119:130)

God gives the reader of the word a light that guides the paths of those who seek Him. We receive understanding through the reading of the word of God. Why do we study and read the Scriptures? To better understand the true knowledge of God's plan and purpose.

We are blessed because we have access to the Scriptures. Today, we have unlimited access to the Scriptures through all forms of media. One hundred years ago, the world had the written Scriptures in the hard cover book. This was available, but it was hardly easily bought or distributed. The Bible was used in the public schools as a core text for learning until the turn of the twentieth century. Today, it is banned from the public schools. In many schools across the country a child can almost get in as much trouble if they bring a Bible and display it publicly, as they would a weapon. Why do you think that is the case? It is sad that we have been reduced to this amoral display and acceptance within the schools. The display of the Ten Commandments are being removed from the courtrooms and public buildings. Why? Because we do not want to be reminded of our sin. If "Christians" would stand firm on the word of God and not waver in their beliefs, then the word of God would not become a classic best seller that is considered a story book for the previous generations. They believe the Word of God is not relevant for today's world and ever changing face of America. If anything, this country and the world need to read the Word of God more today than ever before. It helps us find our true moral compass and stay on the course God, through Jesus Christ, has laid before us.

THE SPIRITUAL CHURCH: WE MUST BE HEARERS OF THE WORD

He who has an ear, let him hear what the Spirit
says to the churches.
(Revelation 2:7, 11, 17, 29; 3:6, 13, 22)

Jesus wanted the churches to have their ears open to listen to Him as He gave them instruction into their salvation. Even the worst of the churches mentioned were not beyond saving. Jesus

Christ has called people to repentance. People in the church are not immune to sinful influences in the world. Those who have ears let them hear what the Spirit is saying to the churches today. Do you understand the implications of the empowerment of the Holy Spirit in the life of a congregation? It is nothing short of miraculous. God has empowered His people to go empower more people to serve Him. Hearing the word of God is primary the establishment and development of the church into the Body of Christ that God has called them to become. The word of God must be at the core of the foundations of a congregation. Without hearing the truth found in the word and brought to the people through the messengers and empowerment of the Holy Spirit, there is no growth into sanctification. As you hear the word of God preached and taught by Spirit-filled Believers, growth can take place in the church. The church today tends to be focused on numbers of bodies and monetary gain as opposed to focusing the call of God through the Holy Spirit. The Lord Jesus Christ will bring the increase in those areas that are needed when the church decides to open their ears and hear what the Spirit is saying to the church.

The parable of the sower in the Gospel of Matthew Chapter 13 gives the reader and hearer a visual perspective into the importance of the word of God. The part it plays in all salvation is crucial in understanding the big picture. In this passage, Jesus presents the word of God as it is spread to various conditions of society. Jesus' understanding into the human nature, particularly in the church, was astounding.

Behold, a sower went out to sow. And as he sowed, some seed fell by the wayside; and the birds came and devoured them. Some fell on stony places, where they did not have much earth; and they immediately sprang up because they had no depth of earth. But when the sun was up they were scorched, and because they had no root they withered away. And some fell among

> *thorns, and the thorns sprang up and choked*
> *them. But others fell on good ground and yield-*
> *ed a crop: some a hundredfold, some sixty, some*
> *thirty. He who has ears to hear, let him hear!*
> (Matthew 13:3-9)

The parable of the sower was one directed to the ones who were hearers of the word. Some were receptive, the word fell on good soil. The other soils were less receptive and were distracted and led astray by the things of the world. The more we close our ears to the hearing of the word of God, the more we will become deaf to the call and purpose of Holy Spirit in our life. The church today is on a decline because of those who do not listen to the word of what is being said. We are also encouraged to test the spirits to see if it is of God. The same thing is true of the word. When a preacher brings the message from the pulpit, the words need to be tested as to the authority and truth from which they are delivered. Also, any teachers among you need to be approved as per the word of God. There are many false teachers out there who can appear to be called and anointed of God but are not. As you hear the word of God, our soil, that is our hearts, needs to be prepared for the word and be willing to live it. Each type of soil that Jesus presents to the people is one that is probably characteristic of any of those who were present when He spoke. This is also including the disciples. As we have said before, even though He spoke to a multitude, including the disciples, He was speaking only to those who were listening with their hearts. This is the only parable that He said, *"He who has ears to hear, let him hear!"* He was wanting to make sure that the ones who were supposed to hear the parable hear it and took it to heart.

THE SPIRITUAL CHURCH: LIVING THE WORD OF GOD

> *Therefore lay aside all filthiness and overflow of wickedness, and receive with meekness the implanted word, which is able to save your souls. But be doers of the word, and not hearers only, deceiving yourselves.* (James 1:21-22)

James was saying here that the importance of the word of God not only is found in the reading or hearing of the word, but more important is that the word of God is to be put in action. The life lived apart from the word of God is one that is dead. The Holy Spirit is one that teaches through the word of God and therefore need to be set as an example in life. The Christian must be set apart from the world in their connection with the world. Even though we are in the world, we are not of the world. The example that the Christian sets should give the worldly person something true and encouraging to have a desire to want in their life. James tells the church to not only be hearers of the word but also be doers of the word of God. A major majority of the church members sit in the pew with little intention of sharing that same gospel with anyone outside of the person sitting next to them in the pew. Many will stay busy within the church and be very active in various capacities, but are truly terrified with going outside the church. We are called to be doers of the word of God. The church is called to be doers of the word of God. Jesus did not set up a church building and invited people to come in and enjoy the emotionally charged worship service. He did not stand and scream and get emotional and animated to the people. Jesus stood among the multitudes, where they were, and spoke the words of God that are truth. If you speak the truth, you shouldn't have to scream and get emotional to grab the attention of the congregation or the people. If you must be emotional and loud, then it does not matter your methods of delivery, they are deaf to your words and they will not be doers of the word. They may go through the motions, but in their heart, they are misled by their own deafness to the word. No matter how much they are preached to and taught, they will never become doers of the word of God until they are willing to open their ears and hearts to the Holy Spirit and the word.

For if anyone is a hearer of the word and not a doer, he is like a man observing his natural face in a mirror; for he observes himself, goes away, and immediately forgets what kind of man he was. But he who looks into the perfect law of liberty and continues in it, and is not a forgetful hearer but a doer of the work, this one will be blessed in what he does.
(James 1:23-25)

The word of God is given to be shared with others. The responsibility of the Believer is to live according to the word of God. The word of God is truth and that truth will set you free. James says that those who are hearers only and not doers is like a man observing his natural face in the mirror, then turns immediately and forgets what kind of man he saw. The word of God makes us reflect on our true face in relation to God. What do you see in the mirror as it reflects your spiritual strengths and weaknesses? Do you see the flaws in your walk with Christ? Are you willing to change and live a life as a doer and not just a hearer only? James was very pointed in his approach and concern for the church and the direction it was falling. He is say here that the one who is a doer of the word is blessed in what he does. The Holy Spirit will the work of the hands of the faithful who pray and work per the word of God. This is blessed! You will be blessed in all you do and say. We cannot do anything on our own.

The church wants, in many cases, to take the world by storm by giving the world what they want rather than what they need. I am not a teacher or preacher who seeks to tickle the ears of the congregation to make them feel good about themselves and therefore justifying any sin as the responsibility of the devil. Any decisions made by an individual based on their beliefs are owned by them. The people and the leadership of those people are held to a higher standard and responsibility to the truth as God sees it. The church needs to take responsibility of its actions and turn back to the Scriptures and rely on the Holy Spirit for guidance. We need to consider the perfect law of liberty. This does not mean to become liberal, tolerant and accepting of everything. This means that the law of liberty refers to the mercy and grace because of Jesus Christ and His sacrifice. We should strive to live a life apart from sin. Therefore, we need doers of the word and not hearers of the word of God only.

THE SPIRITUAL CHURCH: KEEPING AND LIVING THE WORD OF GOD

We then who are strong ought to bear with the scruples of the weak, and not to please ourselves. Let each of us please his neighbor for his good, leading to edification. For even Christ did not please Himself; but as it is written, "The reproaches of those who reproached You fell on Me." For whatever things were written before were written for our learning, that we through the patience and comfort of the Scriptures might have hope.
(Romans 15:1-4)

The foundation of who we are as Christians is seen in the Scriptures. It is through the power of the Holy Spirit that we can serve the Lord and be holy in the presence of a Holy God. The blood of Jesus was the sacrifice once and for all. We, as the Bride of Christ, need to be focused on the task at hand. Jesus told us to love one another as He loved us. Are we truly loving one another in the love of God or for our acceptance? The call is for us to bear one another's burdens and pray for one another. The early church loved one another unconditionally. Are we looking to the Lord Jesus for guidance and strength? Therefore, the Holy Spirit was poured out on the disciples on the day of Pentecost. The beauty of it all is found God's mercy and grace. At the base of it is forgiveness. When Jesus was on the cross, He looked to the Father in heaven and said "Forgive them for they know not what they are doing." Also, when His time had come, He said "It is finished!" and gave up the Spirit.

I beseech you therefore, brethren, by the mercies of God, that you present your bodies a living sacrifice, holy, acceptable to God, which is your reasonable service. And do not be conformed to this world, but be transformed by the renewing of your mind, that you may prove what is that good and acceptable and perfect will of God.
(Romans 12:1-2)

We are to present ourselves as living sacrifices unto God. This is to give yourself over to God totally and completely. The Christian cannot holy and acceptable before God apart from the transformation that is achieved by the work of the Holy Spirit. If you want to be considered set apart from the world as a congregation and a people of God, then you should be transformed and renewed in the way you think and the way that you live. It is crucial that the congregations of Jesus Christ our Savior stand firm together in one accord with boldness, power and authority. The authority and power is only found in the Holy Spirit. Living as a sacrifice before God means to complete surrender yourself to the Holy Spirit and

His guidance. Considering that we are empowered knowing that we are saved by grace through faith in Jesus Christ our Lord!

WHERE DO WE GO FROM HERE?

As a congregation of Believers in Christ, we need to evaluate the condition of the spirit among our people. Is the spirit a spirit guided by the Holy Spirit and truth or is that spirit a one of bondage? Even though a church is growing, does not mean that it is healthy. The health of the church is seen in the heart of the people of the church. As the Apostle Paul said that within the Body of Christ is contain a great diversity of members. Within that diversity there must be unity and strength. This can only be achieved by allowing the Holy Spirit to work throughout the hearts of all members of the Body. The Bride of Christ must be found without blemish. Are the congregations of the faith in Jesus Christ truly without blemish? Continue to take to heart the teachings of the seven churches of Revelation. We need to consider that from the time Jesus taught His disciples in His first recorded sermon, conditions in the Beatitudes. His concerns for the churches in Revelation Chapters 2 and 3 can truly be warranted. How does the church today fit into the overall big picture found in the entirety of the book of Revelation? Jesus said that narrow is the way that leads to eternal life.

REFLECTIONS ON THE CONDITION OF YOUR CHURCH

1. Is the church taking the path of least resistance or are we holding fast to our faith? How is your spiritual health and the health of your church?

2. How is your church going take what you have learned and go forward?

3. Is your church willing to take the necessary steps to move from being the average church to the true Body of Christ? How?

4. What is the plan for growth in your church? Does it include total surrender of all things related to the church to the Will of God?

Let Us Pray:

Most Gracious Heavenly Father, continue to lead and guide Your people into holiness that we may give You glory, honor, and praise for evermore. In the name of God the Father, God the Son, and God the Holy Spirit. In Jesus' Name, Amen

CHAPTER 9

IS THE BRIDE OF CHRIST READY FOR THE BRIDEGROOM?

Watch therefore, for you do not know what hour your Lord is coming. But know this, that if the master of the house had known what hour the thief would come, he would have watched and not allowed his house to be broken into. Therefore you also be ready, for the Son of Man is coming at an hour you do not expect.
(Matthew 24:42-44)

The most talked about and theorized topic in Scripture is the end times or the Apocalypse. Most look at the writings found in the book of Revelation and various other writings in Paul. The truly astute student of the word of God studies various Old Testament books like Daniel, Isaiah, Jeremiah, and many other prophets and their writings. Many even do extensive studies into the Psalms. These are all pieces to the puzzle that is the whole of Scripture. The point is that regardless to how much you read the prophetic writings, you must look to the Holy Spirit as the one that guides you into the understanding of Scripture, whether it prophetic or life lessons.

Because people, even in Jesus' day, were obsessing over the end of days, He felt that He needed to address the concerns of the people before speculation gave birth to chaotic rumors. In this chapter in the study of the church and its condition, I will raise more questions than answers as to where we are as a church and Bride of Christ. Is the Body of Christ (Church) ready for His return? Are we truly without blemish to be presented as a bride to the Bridegroom? If not, then what do we need to do to prepare?

The parable of the ten virgins gives us a glimpse into the human nature and the various assumptions that are made concerning the return of Christ. There is a belief that just because you said "yes" to Jesus, this means you are finished. It is only the beginning. This parable gives the people a subtle view of human nature that we so readily take for granted.

The opening Scripture is setting the stage for the various parables that follow. Jesus wanted to be clear as to what was going to take place and that they need to be ready. The intent of this part of Scripture and the teaching of Jesus was that His disciples and various followers would not become consumed with "when" He will return, but they would be more focused on their relationship with Him and to be ready spiritually for His return. We as Christians should be preparing daily from the moment we are saved to the moment we are with Him in eternity. Remember that Jesus said that narrow is the way that leads to eternal life and broad is the path that leads to destruction. We need to be mindful and focused in our individual lives so that when we come together we will be united, pure and holy before a holy God. Jesus tells us to actively watch. This does not mean that we stand there looking to the sky with our mouths open waiting, not doing anything. James says that we must be doers of the word and not just hearers only (James 1:21–27). The Christian life is about active pursuits of the Truth of God in obedience to the call on our lives.

Jesus uses the analogy of the thief that comes at a time that you are unaware. If you are not prepared mentally for the thief, you will not be physically prepared either and he can overtake you. But if you are prepared for Jesus spiritually in obedience to His call, then you will be ready when He returns. Otherwise, you will be left behind. Looking at the parable of the ten virgins, let us see how He teaches His disciples concerning their preparedness. This is a classic parable of the arrogance of many people drawing assumptions and having presumptions concerning His return in the church today.

> *Then the kingdom of heaven shall be likened to ten virgins who took their lamps and went out to meet the bridegroom. Now five of them were wise, and five were foolish. Those who were foolish took their lamps and took no oil with them, but the wise took oil in their vessels with their lamps. But while the bridegroom was delayed, they all slumbered and slept.*
> (Matthew 25:1-5)

The ten virgins all are representative of the church. Five of them are wise and are prepared for the call. The other five were under the belief that they were good and that was enough. How many "Christians" in the churches today are truly under the deception that they handle everyone else and not themselves. How many people in the church today are weakening the spiritual readiness for His return by their action or lethargic mentality when it comes to spreading the gospel of Christ?

The stage was set for the coming of the bridegroom. Why do you think that it was important that these ten virgins be prepared with extra oil in their lamps? The answer is in the earlier statement of Jesus to His disciples in Chapter 24. They do not know if the bridegroom will be delayed or not. In fact, they are completely unaware at which time He is coming. The ones who took no oil with them assumed that the bridegroom was coming about the time that they would be watching and waiting. The ones who brought oil with them knew that delays were inevitable. Because there was not a set time to which they should look, they were prepared for a lengthy stay. The bridegroom was delayed in the parable and they all slept.

And at midnight a cry was heard: 'Behold, the bridegroom is coming; go out to meet him!' Then all those virgins arose and trimmed their lamps. And the foolish said to the wise, 'Give us some of your oil, for our lamps are going out.' But the wise answered, saying, 'No, lest there should not be enough for us and you; but go rather to those who sell, and buy for yourselves.' And while they went to buy, the bridegroom came, and those who were ready went in with him to the wedding; and the door was shut.
(Matthew 25:6-10)

The bridegroom will come, and we will not know when, so be ready. There will be a day when it will be too late to get prepared. All the life of the Christian and the church that has focused and been involved in things other than those things of God. They will use their oil up on the things for their own glory and not for the glory of God. The day will come upon them, when they least expect it, that the Lord will call the church home. Will we be ready? The foolish virgins were not ready. They assumed that their minimal amount of oil was all that they would need for the wait. When it came to the moment of the call, they realized that their oil was used up. In their panic, they begged to get some of the oil from the others. We handle our own decisions in our spiritual lives and we are accountable to God for those decisions. When a brother or sister in Christ is wavering in their faith and does not listen to the warnings signs, give them guidance but it is their decision to follow the right path. At first look, the wise virgins seem selfish and cold toward the others in their time of need. The point being that the foolish ones knew what was needed for the journey and the possibilities of the night and the call. In other words, we are responsible for our own salvation. No one else can make that decision for us. Somebody else cannot obey God for us. Are you prepared to give account of your salvation and is your heart ready for the return?

Many today in Christianity believe that have enough of Jesus when they said, "I will follow you." Once they accepted Jesus Christ as Savior and Lord, they think that must be all that they need to do. The great misunderstanding in the church today is that they can go to church every time the doors open and that will keep you locked into the Kingdom of God. This is far from the truth. This just means that you enjoy the company of others or that you need your weekly fix of rumor and gossip to spread around. The Holy Spirit has been given to you to continually fill your lamp with the oil of His salvation. Your oil will not empty if your focus is on Jesus Christ. The parable of the ten virgins is a pointed view at the mentality in the churches even today. There are many who are spiritually ready, but there are more who are not prepared. If we are to be the Bride of Christ as the church, then we need to daily turn to Him and live in the Spirit of God.

The five virgins who thought they were ready and were not concerned if there was enough oil for their lamps, the Church still needs to be fully prepared even if the Lord Jesus Christ does not return for another hundred years. It does not matter, because we as the Bride of Christ must be found blameless and without blemish. Is the Church truly holy before a Holy God? The door will be shut one day and those who are not prepared and ready for the Lord's return will be cast out into utter darkness. Eternally separated from God and no chance for repentance. The door was shut to those who thought they had it figured out, but the Bridegroom said to them, "depart from Me, I never knew you!" Always make sure that your lamp is full of oil and shining bright the light of Christ so that you will recognized by the Bridegroom as one of His and be welcomed in as His Bride.

Now when one of those who sat at the table with Him heard these things, he said to Him, "Blessed

is he who shall eat bread in the
kingdom of God!"
Then He said to him, "A certain man gave a
great supper and invited many, and sent his
servant at supper time to say to those who were
invited, 'Come, for all things are now ready.' But
they all with one accord began to make excuses.
(Luke 14:15-18a)

This parable of the great supper gives us a reflection into the mentality of humanity throughout history. Things have not changed today, in fact it has become more obvious. This chapter is a call for the Church to heed the warnings spelled out in Scripture concerning the condition and need for repentance. There are excuses for every occasion. The cross section of culture is found within the doors of any church. The diversity and various levels of maturity in faith is one of the unique strengths of the body of Believers we call the church. More than that, it is the willingness of the Lord God to take all those differences and mold them into a single vessel of beauty that is His glory. The greatest deficit or weakness is that we take that grace and mercy given by God for granted. The greatest excuses in the modern world are those from devout church goers. Some say that "the preacher teaches, but he don't preach, so I am staying home." Others say, "the preacher didn't shake my hand when I was leaving, so I am not going back." The list is continuous. I could write a book just on the excuses I hear of why people quit coming to church.

In this parable of the great supper, we see that the Master sent out a special invitation. One after another, they came up with, what we would consider, valid excuses. But that was the problem. As you will see, the Master will pull His invitation if you do not accept it. Excuses are many. We can think of a thousand reasons why should not go or do something we do not find important to us, but it is not about you, it is about the Master.

The first said to him, 'I have bought a piece of ground, and I must go and see it. I ask you to have me excused.' And another said, 'I have bought five yoke of oxen, and I am going to test them. I ask you to have me excused.' Still another said, 'I have married a wife, and therefore I cannot come.' So that servant came and reported these things to his master. Then the master of the house, being angry, said to his servant, 'Go out quickly into the streets and lanes of the city, and bring in here the poor and the maimed and the lame and the blind.' And the servant said, 'Master, it is done as you commanded, and still there is room.' Then the master said to the servant, 'Go out into the highways and hedges, and compel them to come in, that my house may be filled. For I say to you that none of those men who were invited shall taste my supper.'"
(Luke 14:18b-24)

The servant of the Master did as he was told. He was obedient to the call of the Master and followed His instructions. Are we as faithful as the servant? Look at the various excuses of those friends that He invited to the supper. *The first said to him, 'I have bought a piece of ground, and I must go and see it.'* This is like saying that the piece of land that he bought is worth more to him than the friendship of the Master. *And another said, 'I have bought five yoke of oxen, and I am going to test them. I ask you to have me excused.'* This one bought five oxen and he chose them over his Lord and Master. The oxen will die eventually and return as dust to the earth, the fellowship of the Lord and Master of our life lives forever. *Still another said, 'I have married a wife, and therefore I cannot come.'*

Another excuse, though it seems valid, is what eventually draws us away from our Lord and Master. Even if you know that the Lord Jesus blessed you with the Godliest wife ever formed by God, He must be first in your life. She cannot be your excuse. She is not a good reason for not spending quality time with the Master.

The parable here shows us that we are not God's only choice to act in obedience to the call. If He calls you, He wants you to come for a reason. In the parable, the Master is angered by the refusal of those whom He invited, and He decides to invite all who will come. Though God knew in advance of Israel, the chosen people of God, and their refusal to follow the call of repentance and obedience, He gave them many opportunities for repentance. But, in the end they refused His call and He gave the New Covenant in His Son Jesus Christ for entire world. All humanity could be saved from certain eternal death and invited to eternity with the Father and the Son. Not only that, God also gave us a bonus in His Holy Spirit to live in us to set us apart from the world and the evils in it.

The phrase "the devil is in the details" subtly implies these people who are known to be faithful to others, but, are the lies spun by the devil himself. Consider the possibilities of you, despite how holy you think you are, getting to heaven on your own. The chances are slim to none. In much of modern Christianity, the Lord Jesus and His sacrifice has been taken for granted. The Holy Spirit has been long forgotten and it has been replaced with a showman's form of emotional spiritualist theology. Satan or the devil has truly entered the Holy of Holies, reclaimed the life and Spirit that God gave us and stand on His promises and His commands.

---

*Husbands, love your wives, just as Christ also
loved the church and gave Himself for her, that
He might sanctify and cleanse her with the washing of water by the word, that He might present
her to Himself a glorious church, not having spot
or wrinkle or any such thing, but that she should*

be holy and without blemish.
(Ephesians 5:25-27)

The Apostle Paul was speaking here concerning the Bride as to the Bridegroom. True, this does talk about the relationship that must occur in a marriage between a man and woman but consider the various descriptive ways Paul describes the relationship. First, the husbands must love their wives with a pure love that is focused on God. Christ loved the Church to the point of death on the cross. He freely came down from His heavenly thrown and gave Himself for His Bride, the Church. Secondly, this is the "how" of the progress to purification and holiness. He said that in doing this, He might sanctify and cleanse her (Church). Then, the answer to the how seems so obvious, but it is an arduous process for the most righteous of followers. Paul says that He gave Himself for her so that He might sanctify and cleanse her *"with the washing of water by the word."* The power of the word of God is refreshing to the spirit as well as liberating for the soul. The power in the word is found in the fact that it will sanctify and cleanse the sinner and make them whole in life and holy before a Holy God into eternity.

The "why" is best answered by the understanding that He must do this for the Bride to be worthy to be in the presence of the Father and even the Son. He said that the Church must be presented to Himself as a glorious Church, without spot or blemish. She must be found as holy. Is your church preparing to be among those churches that will be rejected at the door by the Bridegroom or will you be received gloriously into His presence? A church cannot wait to ready themselves for the return of the Lord Jesus. We must look at the spiritual condition of the congregations of all Christianity and know that there are always areas for improvement. To the churches today who think that they have it all figured out and are more righteous than others, sorry, you are deceived. Let the Bridegroom prepare your church for the wedding and rejoice.

---

*And Jesus answered and spoke to them again
by parables and said: "The kingdom of heaven
is like a certain king who arranged a marriage
for his son, and sent out his servants to call those
who were invited to the wedding; and they were
not willing to come.* (Matthew 22:1-3)

This is a truly telling parable about those in the Church who are presently taking the gospel of Jesus Christ for granted. When the king calls, you come, or be left behind. The Father (king) has arranged for His Son (Jesus Christ) to be married. You are invited to the royal wedding, but you decided that you do not want to go. You ignore the call to the wedding or you just decided that you have more important things to do. What do you think the Father's response will be for those who reject the call? Well, it will not end well for them! In this parable, they were not willing to come. Who refuses the invitation of the king? I know that my acceptance of Jesus Christ as my personal Savior came after several years of reluctant rejection of His grace and mercy. The churches, in the end, will not be shown such real grace and mercy by the Father because the true message was there but they chose to twist and pervert it to their own image.

---

*Again, he sent out other servants, saying, 'Tell
those who are invited, "See, I have prepared my
dinner; my oxen and fatted cattle are killed, and
all things are ready. Come to the wedding."' But
they made light of it and went their ways, one to
his own farm, another to his business. And the
rest seized his servants, treated them spitefully,
and killed them.*
(Matthew 22:4-6)

The Father gives us many opportunities to repent and turn back to Him, but eventually, He will say, "Enough!" Usually, you only invite the wedding party to the feast. The wedding party are the family and close friends who are participating in the wedding itself. Because they were friends and family and thought they knew the Son and the Father well enough, they made light of the invitation and went their own ways. Are we, as the Church, taking the invitation of the Father and the Son seriously or are we going through the motions thinking that all is good? He shows us the various responses that are given to the invitation. One, He said, went to his farm. This tells the King that the farm animals and the crops hold a higher regard to him than does the King or His son. Another went away to his business. This told the King that he regarded money above the relationship with the King or His Son. Both reject or at the least take advantage of the friendship and places it in low regard, showing the lack importance or concern for the King and His Son.

The rest of those who were approached by the servants despised and had no respect for either the King or His Son. There are many around the world who suffer and die as they carry the gospel of Jesus Christ to those whom God the Father has called. I do not think those listening to this parable of Jesus expected Him to make such a pointed statement concerning the wedding feast. Truly, a majority of those listening didn't understand the message of the parable. Jesus was bringing out an example in the last of the Beatitudes in Matthew 5:10-12. This is where Jesus told them despite growth in the process of sanctification, they will be persecuted and even die for His name's sake. So, why is it a surprise to us that Jesus would say this in such a definitive manner? Why does the church swat the fly buzzing in the window and ignore the elephant in the room?

THE RESPONSE OF THE KING

But when the king heard about it, he was furious. And he sent out his armies, destroyed those murderers, and burned up their city. Then he said to his servants, 'The wedding is ready, but those who were invited were not worthy. Therefore go into the highways, and as many as you find, invite to the wedding.' So those servants went out into the highways and gathered together all whom they found, both bad and good. And the wedding hall was filled with guests.

"But when the king came in to see the guests, he saw a man there who did not have on a wedding garment. So he said to him, 'Friend, how did you come in here without a wedding garment?' And he was speechless. Then the king said to the servants, 'Bind him hand and foot, take him away, and cast him into outer darkness; there will be weeping and gnashing of teeth.' "For many are called, but few are chosen."
(Matthew 22:1-14; cf. Luke 14:15-24)

We may say that the response of the King was both harsh and cruel. It was not only an act of rejection but acts of aggression toward the King and His Son. In His eyes, this means war! How would you react to this same scenario? Our human mind would condemn the King, but we would also condemn the actions of those whom He invited. The King was not calling them to take part in a ritual act against their will that would lead to their deaths. He called them to a celebration! The King was furious because they refused Him and the invitation, He was furious because they defamed and rejected His Son.

This parable looked at the encompassing view of God in all salvation history. The Lord God is the King and His Son, the Bridegroom, is the Son of God. Those whom He invited were the chosen people called Israel. God had made every effort to invite them because they are the chosen people of God. After being ignored on separate occasions by His people, then they even resorted to killing the messengers and finally when He sent His Son, they killed Him too. God had selected countries that He then allowed to conquer the chosen countries of Israel and eventually Judah because they had turned their backs on Him and would not repent.

The King's next act of mercy was to send His servants into the highways and streets inviting all who would to come to the wedding. As the Church, the whole of Christianity, began to turn to His Son and accept the invitation, He welcomed them into the wedding and later to the feast because we were now friends. We as the Church of Jesus Christ are called to the wedding and the feast. We were not invited because the Jews rejected Him, and He is sulking and chose the second best. The Church as Jesus set it up was planned that way from the beginning. Notice the special wedding garments in the parable that was needed to enter the wedding. The man who had come into the wedding and was not wearing the wedding garments was bound and cast out of the wedding. Why? Because he was not clothed in the white purity garments of the heavenly wedding. You will be rejected and cast out if you are not found worthy to stand blameless before a Holy God. So, is the Bride ready for the Bridegroom?

"Who then is a faithful and wise servant, whom his master made ruler over his household, to give them food in due season? Blessed is that servant whom his master, when he comes, will find so doing. Assuredly, I say to you that he will make him ruler over all his goods. But if that evil servant says in his heart, 'My master is delaying his coming,' and begins to beat his fellow servants,

*and to eat and drink with the drunkards, the
master of that servant will come on a day when
he is not looking for him and at an hour that he
is not aware of, and will cut him in two and ap-
point him his portion with the hypocrites. There
shall be weeping and gnashing of teeth.*
(Matthew 24:45-51)

This is another parable that truly should make you take a hard look at the condition of your church and your role in that church. This parable is taking a hard look at the shepherds of those churches as the leadership and an example for the congregation. The difference in the faithful and wise servant and the evil one is distinctive. The faithful and wise servant does the master's bidding. All that he commands, the servant does. He said that this servant will be blessed. On the other hand, the evil servant is one who does not follow his master's commands. He not only refuses to obey the commands of his master, but he also beats his fellow servants and does what he wants with drunkards. Both the faithful and the evil servants have the same opportunities to serve the master. One chooses obedience and the other disobedience. Which one do you think should be rewarded for service to the master? Neither know when the master will return. The problem is that the master will return at a moment's notice, when they least expect it. The faithful servant chose the wise path and will be blessed and rewarded. The evil servant, on the other hand, will reap the consequences of his actions. This is how it with God and the Church. We must be obedient and faithful to our Lord in all things. One negative rumor or wave of gossip can destroy the testimony of a healthy and vibrant church.

WHAT SHOULD THE CHURCH LOOK LIKE?

---

*Then one of the seven angels who had the seven
bowls filled with the seven last plagues came to
me and talked with me, saying, "Come, I will
show you the bride, the Lamb's wife." And he
carried me away in the Spirit to a great and high
mountain, and showed me the great city, the holy
Jerusalem, descending out of heaven from God,
having the glory of God. Her light was like a
most precious stone, like a jasper stone, clear as
crystal. Also she had a great and high wall with
twelve gates, and twelve angels at the gates, and
names written on them, which are the names of
the twelve tribes of the children of Israel: three
gates on the east, three gates on the north, three
gates on the south, and three gates on the west.*
(Revelation 21:9-13)

The most beautiful vision of the Bride. Do you think that the
Bride has become as John sees her here in this vision? The Church
must repent and turn back to God and His Son Jesus Christ. Jesus
said that He is the way and the truth and the life. He said that no
one can go before the Father except through Him. Therefore, the
Holy Spirit was sent to the people of the Church to empower them
to serve, love and worship Him. The true people of God are those
who believe in the only begotten Son of God and live in the power
of His Holy Spirit daily. These people are also those who are dying
to their self daily and living for Christ.

The angel came to John and spoke to him. The angel invited
him to come and see the Bride, the Lamb's wife. The description
is beautiful and wonderous. He was shown the holy Jerusalem descending out of heaven from God. It had the glory of God around
and within it. The light of the city was like that of the most precious

stone, jasper clear as crystal. It had twelve gates guarded by twelve angels and the names above the gates were the names of the twelve tribes of Israel. These twelve gates of the beloved Bride of the Lamb is guarded by those whom God had proved as the foundations and strongholds of His Kingdom, the twelve tribes of Israel. What does this have to do with the Church today? The Bride of the Lamb *is* the Church and the Bride is guarded by angels at every gate and each gate is proved by each tribe of Israel.

WHERE DO WE GO FROM HERE?

"And behold, I am coming quickly, and My reward is with Me, to give to every one according to his work. I am the Alpha and the Omega, the Beginning and the End, the First and the Last."

Blessed are those who do His commandments, that they may have the right to the tree of life, and may enter through the gates into the city. But outside are dogs and sorcerers and sexually immoral and murderers and idolaters, and whoever loves and practices a lie.

"I, Jesus, have sent My angel to testify to you these things in the churches. I am the Root and the Offspring of David, the Bright and Morning Star." (Revelation 22:12-16)

Jesus said that those who do His commandments have the right to the tree of life and can enter the city gates. He also gives the alternative and that is to choose to not do His commandments and remain outside the gates of the holy city where those who have rejected Christ will be locked out for eternity. Eternally separated from the grace, mercy and love of God and cast into utter darkness. The choice here is clear. Surely, even the atheists, deep in their hearts, are not wanting to enter an eternity that can be eternal nothingness. In the Christian view of eternity for those who reject the Son and the Father, there is eternal damnation and torment in the hell.

The one true understanding that all this book has tried to offer was a look into church as the Bride of Christ. This is a means to open our eyes to the truth according to the Scriptures as to what happens if we stay the course or if we fail and are disobedient to the call of God in our lives. The rewards are great before a holy and just God. Be prepared and stand firm in the faith and follow with all your hearts. Listen to the small still voice of God as He speaks His plan to you and to your church. It is very important that the church be united in one accord and in full agreement as to the vision and mission of God in His Son Jesus Christ through the power of the Holy Spirit. Apart from these, the Bride is not ready for her Bridegroom and will not be received but cast out from the presence of God into eternal torment. So, who do you stand for in your life? Where is your church and how is the spiritual health of your congregation? Is the Bride prepared for the Bridegroom? Remember, the Bridegroom will come as a thief in the night when you least expect it! We must be ready as the Bride of Christ to be received blameless and without blemish to the Bridegroom. Are we ready? Are you ready?

LOOKING AHEAD FOR THE CHURCH

1. Are you ready when the Lord Jesus returns for His Bride?

2. Is His Bride going to be prepared for the return of the Bridegroom?

3. Looking at the beauty of the majesty of the Bride, are we blameless and without blemish?

Jesus Christ is returning anytime, is the church ready? Are we ready?

Let us Pray

Father, You are glorious and worthy of praise and honor. For You are our God and Your Son, our Savior. We rejoice in Your wonderous grace, mercy, and love for Your people and all Your creation. Lord, helps us daily live the lives that bring You glory. Show us, Lord, through Your precious Holy Spirit, how to become the Bride without blemish and blameless before Your to be worthy of Your Holiness. In the Name of the Father, the Son, and of the Holy Spirit. Amen and Amen!

ALSO FROM ENERGION PUBLICATIONS
by J. Hamilton Weston

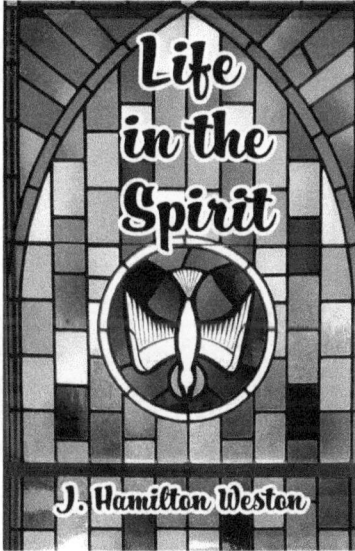

The Believer should be made aware of the power that the Holy Spirit brings when allowed to work in their life.

ALSO FROM
ENERGION PUBLICATIONS

Whatever you believe about the Holy Spirit, His gifts and mnifestations, you need to read this book.

Rev. Mike Roberts
United Methodist Pastor and
District Superintendent, Retired

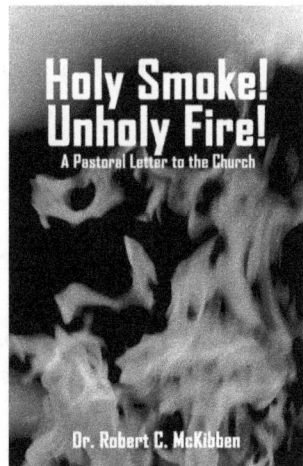

MORE FROM ENERGION PUBLICATIONS

Personal Study

Finding My Way in Christianity	Herold Weiss	$16.99
The Jesus Paradigm	David Alan Black	$17.99
When People Speak for God	Henry Neufeld	$17.99
The Sacred Journey	Chris Surber	$11.99
The Ground of God	Donna Ennis	$12.99

Christian Living

Grief: Finding the Candle of Light	Jody Neufeld	$8.99
Crossing the Street	Robert LaRochelle	$16.99

Bible Study

Learning and Living Scripture	Lentz/Neufeld	$12.99
From Inspiration to Understanding	Edward W. H. Vick	$24.99
Luke: A Participatory Study Guide	Geoffrey Lentz	$8.99
Philippians: A Participatory Study Guide	Bruce Epperly	$9.99
Ephesians: A Participatory Study Guide	Robert D. Cornwall	$9.99

Theology

Creation in Scripture	Herold Weiss	$12.99
Creation: the Christian Doctrine	Edward W. H. Vick	$12.99
The Politics of Witness	Allan R. Bevere	$9.99
Ultimate Allegiance	Robert D. Cornwall	$9.99
History and Christian Faith	Edward W. H. Vick	$9.99
The Church Under the Cross	William Powell Tuck	$11.99
The Journey to the Undiscovered Country	William Powell Tuck	$9.99
Eschatology: A Participatory Study Guide	Edward W. H. Vick	$9.99

Ministry

Clergy Table Talk	Kent Ira Groff	$9.99
In Changing Times	Ron Higdon	$14.99

Generous Quantity Discounts Available
Dealer Inquiries Welcome
Energion Publications — P.O. Box 841
Gonzalez, FL_ 32560
Website: http://energionpubs.com
Phone: (850) 525-3916